More Praise for
Meditation and Relaxation in Plain English

"This book speaks to the reader in clear language and a warm voice. It is a good and friendly introduction for exploring the landscape of the inner life."
—Dr. Jeff Brantley, author of *Calming Your Anxious Mind*

"The book does a particularly good job of conveying the spirit, depth, and promise of meditation in a way that is accessible to those raised in Western cultures. The progression of practice instruction from focus on the breath, to cultivating a good heart and transforming difficult situations, provides a powerful step-by-step guide to meaningful meditative practice with a range of options available so readers can individualize their own practice. This book will be particularly useful for new practitioners and those interested in teaching meditative practice to others in clinical and other settings, although it will also help refresh and renew those with a more established practice."
—Professor Lizabeth Roemer, co-editor of *Mindfulness and Acceptance-Based Treatments of Anxiety*

"There's a very large and growing body of scientific research on the medical and psychological benefits of relaxation exercises and meditation. Until now, though, it's been difficult to find a clear, accessible book that introduces readers to the whole range of exercises from this inner science of training the mind. Sharples' book provides clear, practical, understandable guidance to methods for physical relaxation, training attention, increasing mindfulness, visualization, healing meditations, and increasing positive emotions."
—Lorne Ladner, author of *The Lost Art of Compassion*

publisher's acknowledgment

The publisher gratefully acknowledges the generous help of the Hershey Family Foundation in sponsoring the printing of this book.

Meditation & Relaxation

IN PLAIN ENGLISH

BOB SHARPLES

Wisdom Publications • Boston

Wisdom Publications, Inc.
199 Elm Street
Somerville MA 02144 USA
www.wisdompubs.org

Library of Congress Cataloging-in-Publication Data
Sharples, Bob, 1944-
  Meditation and relaxation in plain English / Bob Sharples.—1st Wisdom ed.
      p. cm.
  Includes bibliographical references and index.
  ISBN 0-86171-286-2 (pbk. : alk. paper)
  1. Meditation. I. Title.
  BF637.M4S52 2006
  158.1'2—dc22

                                    2005036442

ISBN 0-86171-286-2
First Wisdom Edition
09 08 07 06 06
5   4   3   2   1

Cover design by Suzanne Heiser
Interior by Alison Lara

table of contents

preface

My own tentative beginnings with meditation occurred more than twenty-five years ago. At that time I was looking for something to help ease the confusion and distress I felt. I was fortunate to find my way into the presence of some very wise and kind teachers in the Tibetan Buddhist tradition. Their guidance and the practices they introduced me to have formed the focus of my meditation practice ever since.

In 1991, I started working with cancer patients and their families. Most of the work took place in intensive ten-day residential programs. The programs focused on helping the participants become confident in using a wide range of self-help strategies, with the emphasis on meditation, attitudinal change, positive thinking and healthful diet. This work filled my life for eleven years and was to be another powerful influence on my understanding and practice of meditation.

Working with seriously ill people challenged me to find the language and the methods to explain and introduce the practice of meditation to people whose primary motivation was a simple but passionately held one: to use meditation as a tool for physical healing. As a result, I was regularly privileged to witness the most extraordinary transformations in people's lives, sometimes at the physical level, and more frequently at the more subtle levels of spiritual, emotional and psychological healing. These people were doing a lot of diverse activities to help themselves, yet they often ascribed their physical changes and their inner transformations to the practice of meditation.

When the focus is primarily on physical healing, "balance" is a key word that helps to describe the mystery of meditation and its application to healing. Meditation practitioners often feel they have tasted grace—often called bliss in the East—when they first experience a deep harmony and balance in their meditation. The feeling of balance comes from experiencing in meditation that for a while everything in life is at rest and simply in its place: the body relaxed and at ease, the mind calm and peaceful. This state of balance is not one we can easily stay in at the start—the world calls us back all too soon; but it is possible to bring back a feeling of equilibrium that can flow out into our daily life. This sustained experience of equilibrium is the feeling most commonly described by people in the early months of their meditation practice. Meditation can give us a tool to sit more easily in the midst of our life, like a child balancing effortlessly on a seesaw.

In the early years of practice my teachers went to great lengths to remind me that the practice of meditation is not a quick-fix tool or spiritual Band-Aid for easing pain and distress (although it frequently seemed that way to me early on). Again and again they would say, look at your pain, look at your confusion and distress, don't waste your problems, use them to begin to transform the mind. Pema Chödrön, a wonderfully insightful Buddhist teacher, puts it succinctly when she says that meditation is not an improvement plan.[1] The great meditation lineages stress that meditation is not something you do in order to become a holy person or a great yogi or even a meditator. The goal is nothing less than a complete transformation—a commitment to realize through long arduous practice one's deepest potential.

S. N. Goenka, the Burmese Indian meditation master who has done so much to introduce vipassana meditation to the West, frequently refers to his teacher's offhand dismissal of him when he said he wanted to learn how to meditate to fix his migraines. His teacher said that of course meditation could help fix his migraines but to use it merely for that end would be a misuse of the practice when it had so much more to offer.[2]

If meditation is not primarily a quick-fix way of achieving instrumental goals, then what is it? This is a key question for you to reflect on continuously as you read the book. From a Buddhist perspective, a central tenet of meditation practice is that motivation is everything. You are urged to check your motivation regularly throughout the day; to be clear about motivation at the beginning of, during and at the end of every action, even every thought. In the Christian monastic tradition the hours of the day were divided into different practices designed to bring the monk or nun back constantly to an awareness of God's unwavering presence.

My hope is to introduce the practice of meditation to as wide an audience as possible. I have not written about the theory of meditation, principally because I do not feel myself properly qualified to do so. Many books written by great scholars and exemplary practitioners are available today. (See the bibliography on page 167.)

My goal was to write a book free of jargon, dogma or doctrine about some aspects of the "practice" of meditation, and particularly about how to make a start in that practice. I have been a practitioner of Buddhist meditation for twenty-five years. The structure of this book and most of the techniques presented come from that source. In writing this book I am not suggesting that this is the only way, or even the best way for everyone. It is the path that has shaped my practice and for me it has been a rewarding journey, with many unexpected delights.

acknowledgments

Many people have contributed to my understanding and practice of meditation. First and foremost are my teachers: Venerable Lama Thubten Yeshe, Venerable Lama Thubten Zopa Rinpoche, Venerable Geshe Däwa, Venerable Geshe Doga and Lama Choedak Rinpoche. I dedicate this book to them with gratitude and respect.

I would like to thank Ian Gawler and the many colleagues and staff with whom I was privileged to work during my eleven years at the Yarra Valley Living Center. My particular thanks go to the many, many patients and clients who have shared with me their struggles, triumphs and losses. In essence, this book is my attempt to combine the Buddhist meditation practice that came as a gift from my teachers with the efforts of thousands of people to embrace the practice of meditation in their time of crisis.

I would also like to thank my friends and colleagues for the conversations, debates and arguments that helped refine my own understanding over the years. Thank you to my wife, Jenny, who patiently committed my handwriting to the word processor and also provided a valued critical voice. Thanks also go to Alison Ribush and Magnolia Gee of Lothian Books who patiently supported and guided me in the writing process.

And lastly, my thanks go to my parents, my wife and my sons for being a constant source of love in my life.

chapter 1

Why Meditate?

The question "Why meditate?" like all important questions, has many layers of response. As your meditation practice deepens I invite you to be curious and surprised about how your answer will evolve. Meditation is above all an inner art; it requires a willingness to cultivate a turning inward and resting in that inner arc, that inner focus. At the beginning of your practice when you are building confidence and skills it also requires a willingness to rest in a non-doing state, not trying to fix anything; rather, patiently cultivating a different relationship with yourself and, flowing from that endeavor, with the world you inhabit.

In the Western world most of us are addicted to doing so many things. In many ways our contemporary world implies that we are what we do. Compare that with the sentiment expressed in the title of one of the books by the wonderful meditation teacher Ayya Khema, *Being Nobody, Going Nowhere*. In the Christian mystic tradition there is an observation by Meister Eckhart, a fourteenth-century German mystic, that there is nothing more like God in the universe than silence.[1]

Meditation can be powerfully and very directly helpful in ameliorating, even fixing, many of the critical life problems faced by all of us, at least temporarily. However, what frequently seems to happen is that the meditator runs out of puff: the practice becomes boring, tedious, lonely, even scary, or the practitioner feels that they are not "getting it" any more (if they ever did "get it"). All the obstacles and failings so commonly experienced by meditators come back to the failure to keep grappling with this essential question: Why meditate? I can always get a laugh of recognition in a group with the observation that just as the Western world is riddled with failed Catholics, it is also increasingly becoming riddled with failed meditators. I suspect that this pervasive feeling of failure with the practice of meditation is quite unknown to Eastern practitioners.

Why then are we Westerners so hard on ourselves when it comes to the practice of meditation? Again, it comes back to the question of motivation. Because meditation is such a profoundly quiescent, solitary, inner state, it is bound to fail if it is being done to fix a problem. This is even more likely to happen if the practice is being used to escape from pain, sorrow or confusion, or to put a spiritual bandage over it. But, you might interject, isn't that why we come to the practice, because the pain of life has pushed us there? That too is true. A fundamental truth about meditation is that if you do it diligently and with a good heart it will open you even more to your own pain, sorrow and confusion, and then it will open you to the pain, sorrow and confusion of the whole world. And, let's face it, if you come to meditation to fix yourself, you probably feel that you have got enough problems without having to take on a whole lot more.

So, why meditate? The answer is bigger and more challenging but also more delightful than we could ever contemplate at the beginning. You must bring all the parts of yourself to the practice of meditation; but you don't have to "fix" yourself. It is enough to find the patience and perseverance to sit with all these parts of yourself, which is the goal of all the practices presented in this book. The Eastern view suggests that we are okay just as we are—we already have "Buddha nature." It might be obscured but it is there: it is the ground of our being. Our problem is that we don't know it, or at best we know it as a theory but it is not real to us.

After years and years of practice, trying hard to fix myself, trying to feel okay about myself, I was sitting in yet another meditation course, giving it my best shot again, when I heard the teacher say the words, "Meditation is about making friends with yourself." That was all he said, yet a wave of deep relief and gladness flooded through me. I am sure a variation of these words had been spoken often before, but I had not heard them till that moment. Could it be that simple? Meditate to make friends with yourself, the lama had said, and this was for me then, and remains so still, the most eloquent expression of the simple and unaffected grace that can flow into our lives from the practice of meditation. Don't meditate to fix yourself, to heal yourself, to improve yourself, to redeem yourself; rather, do it as an act of love, of deep warm friendship toward yourself. In this view there is no longer any need for the subtle aggression of self-improvement, for self-criticism, for the endless guilt of not doing enough. It offers the possibility of an end to the ceaseless round of trying so hard that wraps so many people's lives in a knot. Instead there is now meditation as an act of love. How endlessly delightful and encouraging.

Meditation as an act of love, as a way of befriending oneself, is such a radical departure from the array of self-improvement projects that are presented in the media and in the life stories of the famous, the successful and those who have prevailed over an affliction or crisis. This being said, the question of utility still hangs in the mind: how can this act of befriending oneself help us to heal; to feel more relaxed of body and mind; to become calmer; to deal with anger, panic and depression; to address our spiritual hunger? The answer to these questions is beguilingly simple: everything is softened by this commitment to friendship; it is only when we can be a friend to ourselves that we can be a friend to the world. On his constant travels the Dalai Lama reiterates like a mantra, "My religion is kindness." Perhaps it really is that simple. In the Jewish wisdom traditions they have a three-line saying that beautifully echoes this idea of befriending yourself: "If I am not for myself, who will be? But if I am for myself alone, what sort of person am I? If not now, when?"

At the end of his short ministry, Christ said to his followers, "This is what I ask of you: that you love one another." Clearly this is easier said than done! How then do we do it? This is the theme we will explore at length: how we can, by beginning with this most elegant and uncomplicated understanding, establish a base for the deepest transformations at the physical, emotional, mental and spiritual levels.

From a Buddhist perspective, the highest possible motivation one can have, from the very first moment of practice, is the motivation of universal altruism—a wish to attain the fully awakened state because that is the best way to help others. I can still hear my first teachers saying, "Please do your practice, do your work. There are so many beings waiting for your love, you mustn't let them down." When I first heard about this level of motivation, I was deeply affected by its purity, nobility and vastness of reach. I saw living examples of this in my teachers. It still inspires me and forms the basis of my daily practice. But after a decade of diligent practice I knew that I was still as estranged from myself and the needs of those closest to me as I had been at the beginning. It was into this space in me, this void in my practice, that the teacher dropped such a liberating phrase all those years ago.

The difficulty with universal altruism is that it can become a Buddhist "motherhood statement"; it can be an entrapment instead into a feeling of universal paralysis. Looking back, I can see that while I was mouthing the words, I was stuck in the attitude of hopefully crossing my fingers and wishing it were so. I needed the gentleness and the kindness of that invitation to bring it home to myself and I needed to be ready to hear and respond in a practical way. The essence of this realization was that if I was ever going to help others it would only come when I was able to be deeply kind and accepting toward myself. In accepting myself in this way I could then begin to relax into practicing kindness, person after person, without feeling lost in the seemingly unachievable invitation of universal compassion.

I hope this book will give you some tools to deepen your cultivation of kindness and compassion.

chapter 2

What Is Meditation?

All the great meditation traditions have as a fundamental premise the understanding that the mind determines the quality of our life. This view is succinctly expressed in the understanding that it is not *what* happens that is important, but *what we do* with what happens. Reflect for a moment on a common experience: when we are happy we tend to see the world as bright and full of possibilities, but when we are down most things look grey and colorless. Shakespeare understood this well when he had Hamlet exclaim, "There is nothing either good or bad, but thinking makes it so."[1] In the East they take this idea further with the view that everything is the *creation* of mind.

Meditation is essentially a practice for training the mind. There are two implications of this. Firstly, it assumes that the mind is poorly trained, if it is trained at all. Secondly, it asserts that the mind can be trained in a positive and helpful way. This is something you will need to check up on for yourself. Having a mind in need of training does not mean that you are unintelligent or witless or stupid; it is not about your intellectual abilities. The old meditation traditions say that the mind is poorly trained because it is dominated by ignorance and delusions, which arise from our incorrect understanding of the nature of things. We often notice this untrained and unskillful nature of the mind when we are in crisis. We find it very difficult to stop the seemingly endless cycle of ruminating, worrying, fearing, and planning. And mostly it's to no avail. Many of us notice a deep restlessness and anxiety in our minds when there is nothing for us to do and there are no distractions available. Sitting in meditation can initially be quite alarming because it is often the first time we notice the crazy untamed and restless quality of our mind.

The mind is a non-physical phenomenon with the capacity to know and experience. It changes from moment to moment. We sometimes talk about our stream of consciousness, an idea that expresses the flowing quality of the mind. Each mind-moment comes from a previous mind-moment and gives rise to the next in a seamless flow. The mind contains all that is conscious and unconscious, which includes all our feelings, thoughts, perceptions, dreams, moods, and memories. Being non-physical it is different to the body, yet it is inextricably linked to the body. We know how our thoughts and moods can impact on the body; similarly, when the body is sick or stressed or in pain this can create great distress in the mind.

Molecular scientists are still discovering and describing the molecules that flow both ways between the brain and body in a constant flow of communication. Candace Pert, a prominent researcher in this field, called them "the molecules of emotion."[2] These new insights from science extend our understanding of the extent of our mind-body connection. Because the mind and body are interdependent, it is essential that the body is incorporated into the process of training the mind that is the fundamental focus of meditation practice. Many people initially come to meditation seeking a tool for physical or emotional healing and for them it is helpful to start with the body as the focus of the meditation. Others come to meditation practices specifically for relaxation. In chapters four and five, I outline practices of relaxation, and the way conscious physical relaxation can serve as a gateway to the other kinds of meditations in this book.

THREE TYPES OF MEDITATION PRACTICE

Meditation techniques are presented and taught in three broad categories: *concentration, mindfulness,* and *contemplation.* These categories are discussed below, as is *creative meditation,* which is an amalgam of the three. As you advance in your experience and confidence you may find yourself using all three together in one session of meditation.

CONCENTRATION MEDITATION

Concentration meditation involves training the mind to stay present and focused on an object or activity. In this kind of meditation, you are instructed to maintain a firm but relaxed focus on the object of concentration. When you notice that your attention has moved off the object of concentration, the instruction is to gently bring it back without self-criticism or analysis. The practice involves bringing the attention back again and again. The most common focus for attention is the coming and going of the breath. Other objects or practices traditionally used are an affirmation, a prayer or mantra, a sequence of movements (as in tai chi or walking meditation), a visualized image, a candle flame, or some ritual. This form of meditation practice will cultivate strong self-discipline and mental pliancy and stability. The follow-on benefit of this form of meditation is the ability to stay more concentrated on, and attentive to, whatever task you are undertaking. This skill will bring real benefits to your everyday life. There is a detailed explanation of this practice in chapter six, and below is brief sample exercise.

E X E R C I S E.

ATTENDING TO THE BREATH

Set aside ten minutes to experiment with this category of meditation. Establish a comfortably erect posture. Take three slow, deep breaths and exhale audibly through the mouth. Then focus on the breath moving in and out, breathing through your nostrils if you can. Find a place where you can feel the touch of the breath coming and going in your body. Hold your attention on the feeling of the in-breath and out-breath in that place in your body. Be aware of the full movement of each breath. Whenever you notice your mind has wandered, bring it back to the feel of the breath. A wandering mind is to be expected, so there is no need to judge or criticize yourself when this happens. Be aware of both the in-breath and the out-breath and the tiny pauses between them. Let the breath find its own rhythm without interfering or controlling it in any way. Just stay with it, focusing the mind on the movement and touch of the breath.

MINDFULNESS MEDITATION

Mindfulness is the cultivation of a "choiceless" or "non-choosing" awareness of whatever is happening in the moment. This is awareness without choosing to accept some experiences and reject others, without trying to create any particular state of mind. It is predicated on the meditator having developed to some degree the skill of concentration. It involves being attentive and receptive to whatever is arising within your experience, being fully interested in all aspects of your world. When you become familiar with this form of meditation you will find it a powerful method of cultivating heightened awareness in everyday life, of becoming less abstracted and lost in automatic behaviors and ways of thinking. It can lead to a much fuller engagement in life and a greater openness to awe and wonder. This aspect of meditation practice is discussed more fully in chapter six. Concentration and mindfulness used together can be a powerful method for focusing your life and intuitively understanding and integrating all the parts of your experience.

E X E R C I S E

NOTICING THE BODY AND MIND

Set aside fifteen minutes. Take a few moments to settle your posture, then focus on how it feels to be fully present, to fully feel your presence in the space where you are. Feel the places of contact and pressure between your body and your clothing, the chair and the floor. Be aware of the sounds around you, letting them come and go in their natural symphony. Use your breath as a focus for your attention, but notice any sensations arising in your body, the moods and emotions of your heart, the pattern of any thoughts coming and going. Be present to all these things choicelessly, without getting caught in commentary and discrimination. Whenever you get lost, bring your attention back to your breath without self-criticism.

CONTEMPLATION MEDITATION

This form of meditation is used for analyzing and reflecting on what you have learnt, your ideas and your experience. It has also been called analytical or checking meditation. Use this method to check up on your intellectual understanding of a topic, to sit with it in a quiet meditative way to see if you can transform it into a more direct inner understanding or realization. This practice is also used to cultivate positive mental qualities like patience, confidence, compassion, forgiveness and loving-kindness. Contemplation meditation is often done in a formal way with a guided step-by-step process for going deeper and deeper into the subject. When you become more skilled, practice it in a more relaxed way, reflecting on the subject then resting in a form of spacious awareness to allow the possibility of connecting with a more intuitive inner wisdom. This can help deepen your understanding and integration of the subject you are contemplating. At other times you may find it helpful to study or read about the subject for a while, then close the

book and turn your focus inward to allow a settling and a perco-
lating at a deeper place in your psyche. Use the practice of contemplation meditation to examine deeply ideas that are central to
a spiritual or reflective life, for example, impermanence and
death, cause and effect, and interdependence. The revered Indian
yogi Ramana Maharshi gave his students only one practice: to sit
in meditation and contemplate the question, "Who am I?"[3]
Chapters eight to ten give details of some meditations that use
contemplation.

CREATIVE MEDITATION

Creative meditation is an amalgam of elements from the three techniques discussed above; yet it is helpful to discuss it as a technique
in its own right. This form of meditation focuses on using the
power of the mind in an imaginative and creative way. The subconscious mind is the repository of all our memories, beliefs, and attitudes and if we can find a way to imprint the most powerful images
we can imagine into our subconscious mind, they will have the
potential to powerfully affect our body, mind and actions. In creative meditation you first develop an image you can hold in your
mind that expresses, in the most powerful way possible, the goal or
outcome you want to achieve. The image should have as much of
the color, power, feelings, words, and details you are capable of
imagining. Repeatedly familiarize your mind with the image during
meditation sessions. The goal is to saturate your mind with the
image, almost like a form of positive mental brainwashing. Once
this new goal or belief is established in your subconscious mind
then your conscious mind will begin to act in accordance with it.

The intention of creative meditation practice is simple, yet it has
profound possibilities. With regular practice the image you imprint
can become so deeply embedded in the subconscious mind that it
will continue to work in the mental continuum of the meditator
twenty-four hours a day. Imagery techniques are widely used for
physical healing. In the new discipline of mind-body medicine it is
often said that "psychology becomes biology." A few years ago I

heard a medical researcher make an even more radical assertion: that our thoughts can even affect our DNA![4]

Creative imagery has long been used in meditation practices with a spiritual focus. It is a way of bringing the result the meditator aspires to into the immediate daily path of their meditation practice. For instance, during the period of meditation, you may imagine yourself as being wise and compassionate and skillful; or you may imagine that you have all the qualities you aspire to, then imagine yourself expressing those qualities for the benefit of yourself and others. You might imagine yourself as a universal being with great compassion, or as completely well and healed from disease and extending that healing energy to others.

Christians will be familiar with the use of creative imagery when they participate in the mystery of the Eucharist and in other rituals of the Christian liturgy. Such archetypal imagery has long been used in meditation practices specifically designed for transformational healing, and it is the basis of the Jungian practices of dream interpretation and active imagination. Creative imagery reaches its highest expression in the practices of tantric meditation cultivated by the Hindu yogis of India and the great meditation masters of Tibet.

E X E R C I S E

HEALING MEDITATION

Set aside fifteen minutes to sit quietly and do this simple healing meditation. (A longer version is outlined in chapter nine.) Take a few moments to relax yourself, letting the weight of your body flow down into the chair and floor. Your muscles lengthen and relax, allowing a quality of softening and letting go to flow through your body. Take time to let your mind become more calm and still. Say to yourself, "I am doing this healing meditation for the benefit of myself and all beings everywhere, particularly those who are experiencing sickness at this moment."

Follow your breathing for three or four minutes, allowing yourself to become more and more calm and settled. Then imagine all around yourself a healing presence, letting it take whatever form your imagination presents. Feel that presence deepen. When you are ready, open yourself to draw from it a flowing energy of healing and purification in the form of light. Feel it effortlessly surrounding you; let it be whatever color spontaneously comes. Bask in its energy as it flows around your body and then feel it effortlessly pouring into your body with the in-breath and through the pores of your skin. Imagine it quickly flowing through your whole body, saturating every organ, every space and every cell. Its sparkling luminosity instantly purifies and transforms any disease, depletion, pain, confusion or delusion in your body and mind. Rest effortlessly in the light for about five minutes. At the end of the five minutes affirm that you are completely healed and well.

You may also like to commit yourself to come back to this meditation practice as often as you can. For the last minute or two bring to mind a few people who are sick and troubled whom you would like to share the meditation with. Imagine them, wherever they are, also in the presence of this energy and spontaneously filling with its healing light. Imagine them smiling with delight as they too experience a deep, spontaneous healing. When you are ready to finish, center your awareness again on the simple flow of your breathing for a few breaths, then take a series of deep full breaths as you bring the meditation to a close.

chapter 3

Making a Start with Meditation and Relaxation

Some years ago I came across a remark attributed to Goethe, the great German writer and scientist. He wrote that it is important to be willing to make a start at something.[1] Once a beginning is made, all kinds of other possibilities, unimaginable beforehand, can come into being. Making a start with meditation may be one of the most momentous life decisions you will make. The Buddha certainly thought so. He said that the greatest gift you can give to another person is to teach them to meditate.

In this chapter, I outline some of the things you can do to support your meditation practice once you have made a start. These are the questions I am most commonly asked on retreats and in meditation groups. Knowing about these things will help to create a balanced and safe environment for your meditation. In some books the "How to do it" section can read like a manual or a list of rules that can seem rigid and formulaic. Rules for practice can be found in all the great contemplation and meditation traditions. These rules have been refined and reformulated over centuries of practice. The existence of these rules reminds us that meditation has always been taught as a disciplined and intentional activity. We can take note of the existence of these traditions to inform our meditation practice without being caught up in dogma and rigidity. These old, well-practiced traditions tell us that it is not skillful just to sit in a chair or plonk down on a cushion and hope for the best. It is possible to distill from the great meditation traditions the core attitudes and behaviors that we can use to support and strengthen our meditation practice.

We live in a world of doing, of ceaseless activity. We may be strongly drawn toward the idea of meditation, but can find ourselves at sea with the daily immersion into a state of non-doing. At social gatherings where we meet new people, the most commonly asked question is, "What do you do?" We know that the answer we give will immediately pigeonhole us in our questioner's mind. Yet we generally feel attached to and even defined by what we do. When we start to meditate, all the *doing* parts of our life are put on hold for a while. Initially this can feel very unusual, sometimes even threatening. It is no wonder that people frequently report one or more of three common responses when they start to meditate: falling asleep; becoming restless and agitated; or feeling overwhelmed by the busyness of the mind's mental chatter.

It is important not to be too idealistic about your meditation practice. Meditation is a variable experience. Some days you will find it to be effortless and peaceful; other days you will be so agitated that the best you can do is just stay seated for the duration. It is quite normal for the quality of your meditation to go up and down. There is no reason for your meditation practice to be exempt from the turbulence and change that affects all the other parts of your life. Meditation is not a quick fix, contrary to the many instant strategies on offer in the New Age marketplace. It is a life skill, and like all others you have to learn it the slow, hard way. A deep and sustained meditation practice takes the same effort you would need to put into learning to play the violin or program a computer. To make it even more challenging, there is no one practice that is right for everyone!

Don't be tempted to constantly evaluate your experience against those reported by other meditators, or those you might have read about. After you have checked out the meditation possibilities, settle on a practice that speaks to you, that you can make a commitment to; and, if possible, seek out a skilled teacher to guide you. Then it is up to you. Be aware that the experiences of other meditators can be a source of inspiration for you, but that your experience will be different. Your meditation practice is strengthened for the long haul when you learn to listen to and trust your own unique experience. One of my teachers constantly encouraged me with these simple words: *"Do it, don't judge it."*

BUILDING YOUR MEDITATION PRACTICE

There are a number of ways in which you can build a confident and reliable meditation practice.

BE CLEAR ABOUT YOUR PRACTICE

There is nothing magical about meditation. It is rather naïve to hope it will all happen if you sit quietly, close your eyes and wait. Doing this kind of thing may produce some benefits, but it is not likely to advance your goal of training your mind. It is more skillful to have a sense of what you are going to do and to be clear and confident in the specific meditation practice you are going to do while you sit quietly.

Confidence in your meditation practice can come from a teacher who personally guides you; a practice you have learned from a reliable source or in a group; or a guided meditation that you follow. I've found it helpful at the beginning to settle on one core practice. There is such a plethora of books, groups and instructional material available today that it can initially feel very confusing. You may need to investigate a few traditions and meditation groups before you settle on one core practice. If you take time to do some active market research at the start you will be more likely to find the meditation practice that will be most rewarding and beneficial for you. Once you are clear about your choice, make a start with that practice and stick with it for a while to give it a chance. Give yourself a year or two to get established in a practice. That being said, it is important to review how you are going over time.

Don't keep doggedly doing a meditation practice that doesn't feel beneficial. It's a good idea to keep your focus on three long-term core goals: calming the mind; generating wisdom; and cultivating kindness and compassion. These three are the benchmarks against which you should test every meditation practice.

As your practice of meditation develops, you may find it helpful to find a group to practice with. Most people find that regular group practice helps to reinforce their confidence and commitment. Some people do not like groups, especially if there is a direct or implied pressure to conform to a particular collective view. You need to know and trust what works best for you. However, it is my experience that meditation is an inherently challenging activity, and most of us will be strengthened and supported by finding a place to do a regular group practice. Again, it may beneficial to find a well-trained and skilled teacher with whom you can forge a personal connection. Some meditation traditions authorize very experienced meditators as official teachers in that tradition. The critical thing is to be confident in the meditation practice you do. Having regular support and an opportunity to clarify any problems or confusion that may arise will help you to build that confidence.

Many people have started meditation practice using guided instruction on an audiotape or CD. This can be very helpful. It helps you keep on track and gives you the time frame for the meditation: it tells you when to start, what to do, how to do it and when to finish. The downside is that you can become dependent on the tape and find it impossible to meditate using your own resources. To counter this, it is a good idea even from the beginning to vary your meditation practice so that you use the recording for only some sessions. Even if you find it difficult to do the practice unassisted it is worth persevering. Remember that meditation is also about building your own inner resources of resilience, competence and wisdom. When you have been meditating for some time it is skillful to use guided meditation tapes only as a back-up for days when you feel agitated, low-spirited or fragile. Then it is like coming back to the support of a treasured old friend who will encourage you and remind you to keep going no matter what hardships you face.

It can also happen that over time you become familiar with a range of different meditation techniques, then become confused about just what practice to do each day. In this situation I have found it helpful to do two things. Firstly, stay focused on the practice you have chosen as your practice of meditation. You may need to go back to your original sources and rebuild that focus and inspiration. It is also important to allow your meditation practice to evolve and grow over time; otherwise it can become rigid and lifeless. Secondly, be playful and curious about other meditation techniques you can utilize for more specific purposes. You will find many ideas about how to do this in subsequent chapters.

CLARIFY YOUR MOTIVATION

Motivation both inspires us and impels us to action. The paradox of meditation is that it is both simple and difficult. It is a simple thing to do yet it requires discipline and effort to do it regularly. Clarity of motivation may be the thing that will encourage you to put that regular time aside each day.

If you are going through a health crisis and you have chosen meditation as an element in your healing program, that will be a powerful motivation in itself. You can start each session of meditation with a firm inner focus. An example might be: "This is a time for healing, a time that I give to myself for my healing." I know that many people come to the practice of meditation for help with depression, anxiety, loneliness or a general state of unhappiness. Again, the motivation can be simply and clearly affirmed, for example: "I am doing this meditation practice to calm my mind, soothe my heart and heal my body." These phrases are just suggestions but I hope you can see how powerful and reinforcing it can be to have a clarity of motivation that you affirm at the commencement of each session of meditation. Whatever the life issue that brings you to meditation, you can craft for yourself a simple statement of intent and motivation to begin each session.

An aspirational or motivational prayer is commonly used when meditation practice has a primary spiritual or religious intent. A Christian might begin with the Lord's Prayer, the Serenity Prayer, or some other formal or informal prayer. This may involve supplications to God, Jesus, Mother Mary, the Holy Spirit or the Saints of the church. Similar forms of invocation and prayer are found in the other great theistic religions. A humanist or non-religious meditator might invoke some form of universal energy. In the Buddhist meditation tradition it is common to begin a meditation session by taking refuge and proclaiming an altruistic intent. Refuge implies a safe and secure support, and in Buddhist philosophy this refuge is asserted to be the Buddha, his teachings (the Dharma) and the people who keep the teachings alive (the Sangha). The practitioner then affirms a wish to reach an enlightened state in order to help others more completely.

My teacher, Lama Zopa Rinpoche, once gave a very simple motivational prayer for people going through a health crisis: "First ask yourself, what is the purpose of my life? ... If you think about this question for a while you will realize that the best use of life is to help others. Then think: I am going to do this meditation practice to calm my mind and heal my body so that I can more skillfully help others. That is the purpose, that is the meaning of my life."[2]

Attitude is central to the vitality of our motivation. An attitude of curiosity is crucial to the practice of meditation. This implies a willingness to do the regular formal practice, but without rigid expectations, and with a sense of wonderment: "I wonder what it will be like today?" This attitude can have a freeing effect—there is no need to force the meditation practice; there is no particular state you have to achieve. You sit down and are willing simply to take what you get. Implicit in this is an understanding that life comes the way that it comes, and you can either learn how to flow with it or spend your life fighting and railing against it. This attitude is marvelously described in the Zen tradition as cultivating "beginner's mind." It is said that in the beginner's mind there are many possibilities, but in the expert's mind there are few. Remember: you are never meditating to become "a meditator," or some kind of an expert or holy person. Instead always practice open to the newness of your experiences.

SET ASIDE TIME FOR YOUR PRACTICE

The most commonly asked question about the practice of meditation is, "How long should I meditate?" At the beginning of your practice, less is more skillful than more. If you push yourself too hard in the early months of your meditation practice you can experience difficulties, which can result in feelings of failure. In the long view of meditation practice these difficulties are normal, but they often come unexpectedly and can overwhelm the confidence of a newcomer. It is best to begin with five- or ten-minute periods of meditation practice, then slowly build up to longer sessions. Twenty minutes twice a day is a reasonable eventual goal for busy people. This is a basic maintenance level of meditation. If you want to deepen your practice or if you are meditating to help with a serious life crisis, then you will generally benefit from longer sessions.

You need to be skillful about the time you put aside for your meditation practice. It is easy to do longer sessions and fall into a dull fog-like state or sit with an untamed, restless, churning mind. When you can sit comfortably for twenty minutes, increase the time to twenty-five minutes, then to thirty minutes and so on up to an hour. It is helpful to bring the curious, questioning attitude of a scientist to your meditation practice, constantly reflecting on the question, "What works best for me?" A good measure of your growing competence will be your ability to maintain your focus and awareness for most of the session. We need to build slowly the capacity to sit in meditation for longer periods, remembering that it becomes harder beyond thirty minutes. Many meditation practitioners find that they can sit for longer periods of time in a group, while at home they do best with shorter ones. As your practice deepens you may find, surprisingly, that you want to sit for longer periods of time.

Keep in mind that meditation is a very personal and subjective experience. Each of us will have a different feel for it and aptitude at it. In my work with cancer patients over more than a decade I noted that some of them benefited most from short, intensely focused sessions of meditation, while others seemed to have a deep urge to do many hours of practice each day (although the individual sessions were never longer than an hour). One is not necessarily better than the other—it is a very individual choice. It is important that we do not turn something we are doing to heal and enrich our lives into something that we are ceaselessly failing at.

Many people find that they quickly learn to estimate the time frame for their meditation and intuitively know when the time is up. This faculty will grow in you as you become more experienced and confident. Remember that meditation is not about going somewhere but about learning how to be present and on the spot. You can have your watch or a clock nearby and check when you think it is time to finish, but make a practice of not checking it too often! In the long run, meditation is most beneficial if it is approached as an intentional, disciplined activity.

In its traditional forms meditation was never a feel-good, spacey, time-out kind of activity. Because the fundamental intent of meditation has always been to train the mind, it is generally taught as a discipline requiring perseverance and regularity. It is not a good idea to sit in meditation for "just as long as it feels good." Specify to yourself how long you are going to meditate for and then stick to it. If after the session you feel that you would like to do more or less, adjust your time frame for the next time you meditate. Do not let your meditation be ruled by your moods, your likes and dislikes, or your temper. When you finish your meditation time, be conscious of the coming transition into the hustle and bustle of life. Sit for a few moments longer, breathe a little more deeply and make a simple commitment to take the calmness of the meditation with you into the day.

I am often asked what time of day is best for meditation. For most people the early morning is best: this is a quiet time of the day when you are likely to be physically rested and your mind is not yet agitated by the events of the day. I am a "morning person" so it suits me to get up early; I have found this a great way to bring more discipline and commitment into my daily routine. If you are a person who likes to stay up late, you will probably find that the evenings are the best time for you. You need to know yourself and your routines when you decide when to schedule your regular sessions of meditation. I find that if I don't have my meditation schedule firmly in place it is very easy to be too occupied to remember to do it or too rushed to fit it in. In other words, if you don't schedule it in, you may not get around to doing it.

It is a great idea to write your meditation times in a timetable and stick to them. Let your family and friends know that you don't want to be interrupted at those times. If you do this they will be prepared if you disappear at certain times of the day.

It makes sense to protect the quality of the meditation time you have set aside. Take the phone off the hook, or turn down the ringer and the volume on the answering machine. Tell your loved ones where you are so they don't come looking for you. Put a sign on your door. If you have young children, you may need to plan your meditation times around their activities or ask friends or family members to take them out so you can have a break. Mothers of young children have often told me that they regularly meditate in parked cars because they are the only quiet places around the home. This is a reason why many people meditate in the early morning—it's the one time of the day they can consistently find some peace and quiet.

Remember that even when you are interrupted during your meditation, you still have a choice: you can get angry and frustrated or, more beneficially, you can deal with the interruption, settle yourself and go back to the practice. At other times you may need to be realistic about the situation and compassionate toward yourself. You may decide to stop the meditation session because the interruptions are too intrusive or you have lost your focus and stability. Some days your "monkey mind" may be so active that it makes better sense to go for a walk or make a cup of tea, then come back to the meditation practice if you have time. This can also happen to very experienced meditation practitioners, especially when disturbing life events occur. If this happens frequently you should take steps to apply a little more rigor and discipline to your meditation practice.

Another cause of interruptions to your meditation can be the resentment or even aversion of your loved ones to what you are doing. Your partner, friends, or children may not share your enthusiasm for meditation. They may see it as an avoidance of intimacy or the loss of a time for simply being together. Friends can be suspicious of your motives and see you trying to become a "holy Joe." If this happens it is vital that you address their concerns. Tell your friends and loved ones as simply as you can why it is important for you and ask for their understanding and support. If you fail to do this they may become hostile to your meditation practice and find ways to consciously and unconsciously disrupt your meditation time.

One of the ways to strengthen your meditation over time is to look for opportunities to meditate in more challenging locations: outside in your garden, in a local park, on a bus or train, or while sitting in a doctor's waiting room. These locations and many others offer you an opportunity to test your ability to slow down, soften and turn inward amid the chaos of life; to experience meditation in action. Doing this can help you remember that you are not meditating just to have an easier life but also to strengthen your mind and cultivate your inner potential. Even the busiest activities offer opportunities to use your meditation skills. For example, when you are stuck in congested traffic or at a red light you can use those few moments to come home to yourself, breathe a few mindful breaths and be in the moment. If you extend your meditation awareness and focus in these ways, you can prevent your meditation practice becoming a fixed formula pigeon-holed into a certain time of the day and forgotten about otherwise.

The distress and dislocation caused by serious illness or trauma can also affect your meditation. If you find this to be the case, it may be helpful to use a guided meditation tape or CD, or to practice doing regular short meditations of between five and ten minutes. With practice you can become quite adept at using short sessions like this to maintain your meditation practice no matter what

difficulties you are experiencing. An even more skillful and paradoxical practice at these difficult times is to make whatever difficulty you are experiencing the *focus* of the practice. This involves
focusing on the pain or distressing symptoms and breathing into
them with compassionate awareness, not flinching from the problem but bringing the meditation practice to the help of the problem. There is more about this in chapters seven and nine.

The time you put aside for your meditation practice will be
enriched if you take steps to ensure that you are alert and wakeful
during the practice. Meditating before you eat is simple common
sense. If you meditate on a full stomach your body will be focusing
a lot of energy on digestion. Try to approach your meditation with
a calm mind and a feeling of readiness for what you are about to
do. Don't go mindlessly onto the meditation cushion or chair after
rolling out of bed or coming home from work.

The Dalai Lama has observed that Western people, with our
busy lives and different cultural context, often have difficulty finding enough time each day for a lengthy meditation. However, he
recommends that because we are blessed with regular holidays and
weekend breaks, we make an effort to do some periods of more
intensive practice or retreats each year. As you become more confident with your meditation you can experiment with occasionally
setting aside a half-day, a day or a whole weekend for a more intensive period of practice. During that time, try to cut out distractions,
simplify what you do, and practice being more fully present to the
rhythm of your life.[3]

There are many opportunities in the West to engage in longer
formal retreats in a variety of traditions and settings.[4] When you
are ready for a retreat this can be a great way to go deeper with your
meditation and reinforce your commitment to a daily practice. You
can also do a less formal retreat by going to the beach or the country for a few days and using the time to slow down: turn off the CD
player, the television, and the radio; put aside magazines, books,
and newspapers; allow everything you do to be at a more leisurely
pace. A good friend of mine with a very hectic life takes himself to
the desert for a long weekend once a year. He goes by himself with

a small tent and just sits and walks and ponders. He always comes back deeply enriched by the experience.

CHOOSE A PLACE FOR MEDITATION

You can meditate anywhere. As you become more confident you will find it easier to soften your gaze and turn your focus inward—coming home to the body, to the moment and to the breath—wherever you are. If you do it in a public place, try not to draw attention to yourself. It is best to be modest and discreet in your meditation; after all, you don't want it to be a cause of any further hostility or aversion in the world!

If possible, create a special place for your regular daily meditation practice: a place that is reserved for meditation and other quiet, contemplative activities. This place may simply be a small corner of a room. Ideally it will be a place where you will not be disturbed. I know people who have converted a shed, a loft, or a van for their meditation space. When I first began to meditate I had a young family and I sometimes used a small greenhouse my wife and I had built some distance from the home. If I meditated in the house my children would often wander into the room where I was meditating, plonk down in my lap for a while, then wander off. If I didn't make a big deal out of it they learnt to see it as just something that their dad did. I spent years trying to get up before my children; in the end I just had to give in and learn to live with the occasional "group" meditation.

It is good to make a special effort to keep your place of meditation clean and uncluttered. It can be an external representation of the state of mind you want to cultivate. I strongly recommend that you guard against the room becoming overheated or stuffy. In the colder months it is better to wrap yourself in a blanket than make yourself drowsy in an overheated room.

One of the great losses in our modern secular world is the absence of ritual. Ritual helps to make an activity feel special, and it provides a bridge between the mundane world of ordinary reality and the possibility of a spiritual or transcendent reality. To practice meditation is to be a little more open to the spiritual and the numinous. Many people find it helpful to use a ritual as an entry point into their meditation. The ritual serves to remind them that this is a special time, a time they are setting aside for their inner life, for spiritual practice, for healing, or simply for rest and renewal. I am constantly amazed and delighted at the range of rituals people devise. It can be as simple as lighting a candle or bringing in some flowers from the garden; it can involve elaborate prayers and prostrations in front of an altar filled with holy objects. I recommend you give some thought to creating a ritual that will imbue your meditation with a sense of reverence. There is an old teaching that says, "Invited or not, the gods will always be present." Using a ritual that has meaning for you will help keep the presence of the divine in your awareness.

I prefer to meditate in a place where there is some natural light. I find that my meditation flows more easily in such an environment, or one with very soft artificial light. If I can meditate through the changing qualities of the dawn and dusk I feel more connected to the rhythms of nature. The early evenings are a special time: I love sitting at dusk with my meditation accompanied by the sounds and feelings of early evening and the roosting of the neighborhood birds. When I am away on holidays in the summer I love to go down to the beach or out into the bush at dawn and settle down to meditate wrapped in a blanket and wearing a beanie.

ADOPTING A POSTURE FOR MEDITATION

Posture is important in meditation. It sets the tone of your practice and provides the base for the deepening of experience over time. All the great meditation traditions have detailed and very specific descriptions of the correct posture to adopt for meditation. These instructions emphasize the importance of sitting with a straight back and a balanced head, with the crown of the head uppermost. However, it is also important that you make a start with meditation in a way that works for you. Adopt a posture that is as balanced and upright as you can comfortably manage. Over time you can gradually progress toward a more formal and elegant posture that will support a deepening and maturing of your meditation practice.

Alertness is one aspect of good meditation and a more demanding posture helps to cultivate that quality of alertness.

In the East the common meditation posture is to sit on the ground with the legs crossed with feet on top of the opposite thigh, or with the ankles one in front of the other on the floor. In Japan a kneeling position is often used. In Western countries our renewed interest in meditation has mostly come through the influence and teachings of Eastern masters. These traditions generally assert the importance of sitting in the cross-legged lotus position. In the Hindu tradition it is common to sit directly on the ground. Meditators who grew up in the East seem to be able to do this for long periods of time; however, a cushion is essential for most Westerners as it helps to tilt the body forward so that the back can be more easily kept straight.

The great advantage of the cross-legged posture is its stability. When cultivated over time it can give you a feeling of being strong and unmovable as you meditate. There is an elegant traditional expression of this possibility that can be helpful at the beginning of a meditation session: "I am going to sit strong like a mountain so that my mind can be open like the sky."

The lotus or cross-legged posture is difficult for Westerners used to sitting in chairs. It takes a lot of practice to be comfortable sitting in this position for any length of time. There are many different ways to sit with crossed legs. It is helpful to get a specially made meditation cushion to place under the buttocks. You may need to start with quite a few cushions. Normally the right leg is in front of the left; the goal is to have both knees on the ground. At first you may find it hard to get your knees down, but be assured that as long as your body is reasonably flexible and you persevere this is quite achievable. Only a few very dedicated and flexible Westerners will be able to sit in the full lotus position but there are many other more body-friendly variations of the lotus position that you can try. Remember, the advantage of this posture is that it is the best way to get the body grounded and stable with the back straight and the head balanced.

A compromise between sitting cross-legged and sitting on a chair is to kneel. You can buy or make a little bench that will take the full weight of your body with your legs folded underneath. These kneeling benches are specifically designed for meditation and are sloped forward to help keep the back straight and allow a stable posture. They also take the weight and pressure off the ankles and are much easier on the knees. The bench should be just high enough to allow the folded legs to fit comfortably underneath. You can make a luxury padded model, which is kinder to the buttocks, for longer periods of sitting. Many people find using a bench preferable to the strain on knees and hips caused by prolonged cross-legged sitting. When I was doing long retreats I avoided a lot of soreness by alternating between sitting cross-legged on a cushion and using a kneeling bench.

The good news is that you don't have to sit cross-legged *or* kneel! Many people have very good meditation experiences sitting on a chair or even lying down. If you use a chair it is best to choose a simple kitchen chair or dining chair that enables you to sit with both feet squarely on the floor and your back straight. Aim for an elegant, formal, upright posture; try not to sprawl or cross your legs. The more you push your backside into the chair the more you will be able to maintain a straight back. Avoid chairs with arm rests. Support the weight of your arms in your lap or on your thighs, which also helps the shoulders to relax more completely. Some people sit in a chair that is ergonomically designed to support the back; others sit forward with their sit-bones on the edge of the chair so that the back is not supported by the chair. Personally, I don't find these positions comfortable. You can alternate between sitting cross-legged on a cushion and sitting on a chair if you want to train your body gently to be more accomplished in the cross-legged posture.

If you wish to lie down to meditate you need to be aware of the possibility of falling asleep. Lying on the floor is preferable as a couch or bed is too comfortable and too closely associated in the mind with sleep. I recommend that as you become more confident with the practice of meditation you graduate from lying down to using a chair—unless you have a serious back problem or other health issue that makes it impossible to sit for any length of time. If you do lie down to meditate, rest your arms on the floor alongside your body and avoid crossing your legs. Remember to put a yoga mat or blanket underneath you as it can get very cold on the floor.

I have worked with thousands of cancer patients and people with other serious health problems over more than a decade. Many of them achieved very deep and sustained meditation experiences sitting in a chair or lying down. Some did hours of practice each day; others did only a little, yet they often reported profound experiences, and sometimes even mystical experiences, during their meditation. The point of telling you this is to emphasize the importance of motivation and attitude. While posture is helpful in building the enduring practice of meditation, it is the passionate willingness to do whatever it takes that really makes it work.

There are some other aspects of posture that you should be aware of. Keep your hands soft and relaxed. You can sit with your hands lightly clasped together or resting in your lap or along your thighs. In the Buddhist tradition it is generally recommended that the hands rest either palm down on the knees or in the lap with the back of the right hand in the open left hand, facing up with thumbs touching. In the Hindu tradition it is common to sit with the arms resting along the thighs, hands facing up, resting on the knees, thumbs and forefinger of each hand touching. You can try these traditional methods or work out for yourself what suits you best.

Your head should sit easily in its point of balance if you sit or kneel. The jaw is relaxed, the lips loosely touch, and the tongue rests against the upper palate. The eyes can cause problems for us. We Westerners find it easier to meditate at first with our eyes closed. In our Judeo-Christian culture, prayer and contemplation are normally done with closed eyes. Closing our eyes to meditate feels more natural and connects us with a sense of turning our focus inward. The problem is that when we close our eyes to meditate it is easy to "space out" or fall asleep; it can accentuate the idea that by meditating we are seeking to go somewhere else. In the traditional teachings there are various recommendations, from eyes wide open in Zen Buddhism, to eyes partially open with a soft gaze in Tibetan practices, to eyes closed in both vipassana and the Christian contemplative path. Take time to work this out for yourself. I spent years meditating with my eyes closed but now I find it more beneficial to sit with my eyes partially open with a soft gaze focused on the floor about one meter in front. You may like to vary your meditation by having your eyes open for some sessions and closed for others.

Good posture is also important if you plan to do walking meditation. Just as there is a significant difference between our normal sitting posture and our sitting posture for meditation, there is a difference between our normal walking gait and our walking gait for meditation practice. The aim of walking meditation is to be fully present and conscious of every aspect of walking. Slow down the walking and take each step consciously, noting the lifting, moving and placing of the foot. Walk with the body erect and the head well balanced, looking at the ground in front. Rest the hands in a position that you can maintain for the length of the session, either loosely hanging at your sides or lightly clasped at the front or the back. In some walking meditation traditions the hands are clasped at the chest, though I have never found that position comfortable or helpful.

Many of the traditional forms of meditation go back thousands of years and are based on exotic and esoteric ideas. One aspect of these ideas is posture. It is said that a firm sitting posture helps to keep the mind sharp as well as support the free movement of the subtle wind energy in the body. The idea of chakras and subtle energy channels in the body forms the basis of the Eastern understanding of health and spiritual energy. It is said that this subtle wind energy can flow more freely in the body when the back is straight and erect with the head balanced. There are now many good translations of traditional texts that give detailed explanations about the subtle wind energy, the channels and the chakras. However, be careful not to get so caught up gathering information on the esoterica of meditation that you lose sight of the primary importance of simply doing it.

BUILDING CONFIDENCE AND RESILIENCE IN YOUR MEDITATION PRACTICE

I have found it important not to talk too much about my meditation practice. Meditation is essentially a private and personal experience. Our meditation experiences can also have a vulnerable, tentative quality, like a delicate new bud or a flower slowly emerging. Our experiences can be easily mocked, questioned, or scorned if we talk about them to people who do not have an interest in meditation. Be respectful and nurturing of your meditation experiences, especially in the early years of your practice. Be aware that it is easy to fall prey to pride, inflation and egotism when you try to explain to others these essentially personal and private experiences.

Don't spend too much time analyzing your experiences in meditation. I advocate the no-nonsense, don't-complicate-it school of meditation practice. Again: "Do it, don't judge it." However, you may be fortunate and have a teacher or a meditation community you belong to where it is safe and appropriate to discuss your experiences and seek further guidance.

Sometimes experiences can occur in your meditation that are distressing, confusing or even frightening. These experiences will normally soften and go away over time, especially if you don't run away from them. They may even contain the kernel of new insights and progress for you. Remember, you can always decide to stop your meditation session if things become too difficult. However, if you feel stuck with problems in your meditation practice it is essential that you seek skilled help and advice. We are fortunate that there are many wise and experienced meditation teachers available to us. It is best to find a teacher who belongs to an authentic and tested lineage of practice.

In some cases, one thing you may find helpful is to keep a daily journal of your meditation practice. A short paragraph each day is generally enough. You can record how long you sat, the type of practice you did, the state of your mind and body, the quality of the session, what came up, what was easy and what was hard. You may occasionally want to write a lot more. Keeping a formal journal like this honors the effort you put into your meditation and enables you to get some perspective on how your practice is progressing. Hopefully you will begin to notice that your problems and worries ease, and that other issues arise to challenge and extend you.

The biggest problem with a regular meditation practice is that we can lose heart and feel like a failure or simply get bored. A practical common-sense approach is best. It is very important not to be too idealistic about your meditation: it will improve and worsen, fluctuating like every other aspect of our human experience. It is normal to have good days and bad days, good and bad weeks, months, or even *years*. The best antidote to this ebb and flow of experience is to have a clarity and discipline about your meditation practice. It is also very helpful to have a few books that you can return to for guidance and inspiration and a group with a living tradition of practice that you can join.

Boredom is very damaging to the long-term viability of your meditation practice. You need to address it quickly and consciously. Take steps to "spice up" your meditation time. For example, burn incense, change your posture, sit in a different room, find a place with spiritual or religious connotations where you can be inspired, go outdoors, sit in a more difficult or demanding position, try a new technique, do some yoga or tai chi before you sit, or try walking meditation. Introduce some ritual into your meditation time. Look for sources of inspiration in books, people, groups or a teacher. Be a bit creative in your meditation: sit for longer or shorter periods, open or close your eyes, try a different chair or cushion, treat yourself to a new meditation shawl or a holy picture or object. Seek out ways to build a sense of delight into your meditation as an antidote to boredom.

There is another source of potential confusion and difficulty that is hard to describe because it is so complex. It is succinctly expressed in the Zen aphorism, "The finger pointing at the moon is not the moon, and cannot pull it down."[5] There is a rich and challenging paradox here: we need the discipline to commit to regular meditation practice, and we also need the wisdom to be able to let it go when the time comes, to remain open to change and renewal. The meditation is not the end in itself but the means to an end. Sometimes we can find ourselves stuck in a deep rut of routine and boredom in our meditation. Don't be too attached to the form of your meditation practice. Have the courage and wisdom to reach out to change and grow your practice as you change and grow. Once again, a wise teacher can be very helpful if this happens to you.

DEALING WITH HINDRANCES TO MEDITATION

The biggest hindrance to our meditation is constant intrusive thoughts. This is normal for everyone, and from the beginning you should expect it. The nature of our mind is to think, and it is childish to imagine that we can simply turn that process off when we wish to. Our minds have been almost completely out of control for most of our life. Recognizing this can help us to be practical and patient—it may take us some time and a lot of skillful practice to tame the crazy "monkey mind." My own meditation practice was helped when I came across the instruction that while I *have* thoughts I *am not* those thoughts. When you stop to examine your thoughts you start to see that they have a life of their own, they come and go, generally in a random, idiosyncratic way. Recognizing the constancy of our endless thinking process is said to be one of the early important steps we take on the meditation path. In fact, for many people it is only when they take up the practice of meditation that they become aware of this incessant stream of unexamined thinking and the attitudes that lie behind it.

In the beginning the instruction is to notice this stream of thoughts. The practice is to try and simply let them come and go, without getting caught by them and without fighting or resisting them. Naturally this takes a great deal of practice and I will talk about how to do it in chapters six and seven. It is helpful at the beginning of your meditation practice to free yourself from the idea that in order to meditate properly you must have no thoughts. Instead, establish a different relationship with your thoughts so that over time they can fade more effortlessly into the background. All meditators have thoughts arising during their practice—it's what you do with them that matters. The same can be said for moods, emotions, feelings and physical sensations, although they tend not to have the same degree of intrusiveness that thoughts have.

Another significant hindrance can be the criticism or even hostility of friends and family. I have already discussed how regular meditation practice can take you away from your loved ones, if only for brief periods at a time. They can and often do feel angry and resentful. Friends may worry about you changing. You need to be skillful in how you introduce meditation into your daily life. Keep your practice to yourself if you can; don't make a big deal about it to people you know. If people ask you why you are doing it, try to talk about it in a simple, modest, and unpretentious way. Resist the temptation to start preaching about your meditation practice: do it because it feels right for you.

In the East, hindrances to meditation are taken very seriously. The early Christian Desert Fathers wrote extensively about the recurring hindrances to a life of prayer and contemplation.[6] The beginning meditator is prepared in advance so he or she is not surprised or disheartened when these things come up. The common hindrances are described under five broad headings: desire, aversion, sloth, restlessness, and doubt.

desire

Desire is often described as the "wanting" mind or the "if only" mind. The time spent in meditation can be absorbed in endless fantasies about what we need to make us happy. Our consumerist and materialistic modern world gives enormous emphasis to feeding this desire. The power of desire can be experienced in many forms and in relation to a wide variety of objects: for example, possessions, relationships, reputation, career, achievement, sexuality, body image. Also there are the "if only" desires that can come up about our meditation practice: if only my mind was not so crazy; if only I had a more comfortable cushion; if only my knees didn't hurt so much; if only I had more time. There is really no end to the "if only" cravings that can arise in meditation. It feels so familiar and comfortable to luxuriate in these constantly arising fantasies.

The best antidote is to train yourself to recognize desire when it comes up while you are meditating, note it, and then simply observe it. This takes a lot of practice, but if you persevere you start to notice over time that the desire is not fixed and it soon fades or changes. There are more detailed instructions on how to do this in chapter seven. It is also said that you can lessen the distracting power of the "if only" mind in your meditation by remembering death and impermanence, the truth that nothing lasts, that the things you clutch at will only offer an illusory and temporary comfort.

aversion

Aversion is the opposite of desire—the "not-wanting" mind. It is the mind caught up in feelings of anger, ill will, resentment, rage, irritability, hostility, jealousy, enmity or boredom. These strong negative emotions come up during meditation, and we can become consumed in endlessly repeating and ruminating over our grievances. The best way to soften the power of aversion patiently is to train yourself to see it when it arises and then observe its presence and energy in your body and mind. If you observe it in this way without reacting, aversion begins to loosen its obsessive grip in the mind, and the energy of aversion starts to dissipate. Also, cultivate loving-kindness, compassion and rejoicing as powerful antidotes to these negative states of mind.

The power of aversion to disrupt our meditation comes from the habits of reactivity, partiality and anger that are deeply ingrained in us. It takes years of practice to stop ourselves automatically falling into these instinctive negative mind states.

sloth and torpor

These words are a bit old-fashioned today; we are more familiar with this hindrance being described as sleepiness, postural slumping, laziness, procrastination, and boredom. Sloth and torpor come from a lack of commitment and resolve in our meditation practice.

Don't let your meditation become dull and routine; avoid slumping in the chair or onto the cushion and hoping for the best. Monitor your physical and mental condition so you know what level of effort and concentration you require each time you sit for meditation. Freshen up the room if you are tired; be more assertive and strong in your posture; sit for a shorter time. If you nod off during meditation, you have some choices: stand up and stretch; open a window; open your eyes; take a few long, slow breaths in, hold each one as long as you can and then slowly exhale. Rebuild a sense of specialness and delight around your meditation practice. You can do this through ritual or variation, by seeking out new sources of inspiration, and by making sure your meditation environment is clean and inviting.

restlessness

Sometimes the mind and body can be too stimulated and overwrought with a deep, restless, unsettled energy. If you meditate at these times you can feel a jumpy, nervous agitation. The best thing to do is to confirm your commitment and resolve to your meditation practice and try to sit through it. It is often said that a mature meditation practice is partly about a willingness to sit on your cushion or chair and take what you get. Many meditators find it helpful to burn up some of this energy with some form of physical activity, yoga, running or swimming before they meditate. A period of deep abdominal breathing or some other breathing strategy can also help prior to settling into the meditation session. However, if the restlessness feels unmanageable on a given day it may be more skillful to stop fighting it. Take a break and do something else for that session time: have a quiet cup of tea, walk in the park, or do some more active spiritual practice like saying prayers, reading scriptures, or doing prostrations.

doubt

Doubt can be the most insidious and damaging hindrance if it is left unchecked. Doubt does not relate to a dogma, doctrine, technique or belief system. It is the more deep-seated doubt in your own ability: a doubt about whether you can make progress in calming and training your mind and achieving more of your innate potential. In contemporary society many people are hampered with feelings of low self-worth; it almost seems to be a disease of modernity. The best antidote to the hindrance of doubt is to find people, books, ideas, and teachers that inspire you to think big about yourself, and then to follow up these sources of inspiration.

PRACTICE WITH KINDNESS, DILIGENCE, AND CURIOUSITY

Practicing meditation can be a way of cultivating kindness toward others—but it is also important that we never falter in extending this kindness to ourselves. The Buddha said that our mind has been out of control for millennia, so it's silly and childish to expect that it can be quickly quieted and tamed. We can lighten up and commit ourselves to the long haul. I once heard it said that meditation is really about remembering to come back. The essence of the practice is to come back again and again to the present moment. This requires great patience and diligence because the implication is that most of our life we have been lost, or at best only semi-present. One Christian saint said that even if you have to bring your mind back to the subject a thousand times during your practice your time would still be well spent.

Each time you sit, come back to beginner's mind: "I wonder what it will be like today?" Let your meditation lead you over time. There are many books of instruction and wise traditions that you could follow, but there is only one you. Meditation should not be you trying to squeeze your round-pegged self into a square hole of belief or dogma. Meditation is a tool to help you embrace and nurture your own unique self; to wrap it in love and deep affection; to offer that love to all beings; and, over time, to cultivate the fully awakened mind. The sobering reality is that in order to do this you need to cultivate the old-fashioned virtues of discipline, commitment, regularity and perseverance. In the following chapters you will discover some of the ways to do that.

chapter 4

Starting with Relaxation

In the 1960s a powerful cultural change began to sweep through the Western industrialized world—this period was the start of an era of sex, drugs and rock'n'roll. With it came the beginnings of a great diaspora of Eastern mysticism and spirituality. Yogis, lamas, roshis and gurus began to emerge in Western consciousness. This movement continues to gather pace and adherents. Ram Dass wrote about his own extraordinary meeting with this movement in the book *Be Here Now*; how it transformed him from a drug-addled ex-Harvard professor to a leading practitioner and teacher of this new Eastern spirituality, with its emphasis on meditation.[1]

However, problems soon emerged for the legions of aspiring meditators. When the bliss-trip passed, when the holy guru moved on, there they were, stuck in their same old rut. The meditation became boring and repetitive, and it seemed impossible to get back to the first heady experiences. It just wasn't as interesting as sex, drugs, and rock'n'roll. So after a time it was back to business as usual. What was the problem?

The truth of the matter was that we in the West spoke a different language to the Eastern masters—a different language of experience from a very different cultural perspective. For the Eastern teacher and practitioner it was natural and effortless to sit and practice meditation for long periods each day. They knew instinctively, from the depths of their culture, that meditation was a sustained act of turning inward. They had made their peace with the hindrances and distractions; for them meditation was an effortless process. Not so the Western aspirants, struggling with the "monkey mind," the restless, often pain-wracked body. Even more distracting was the Western consumerist attitude: "If it's no good here I'll try another teacher, or center, or tradition. Perhaps Sufi dancing is what I should be doing or visiting an ashram in the Himalayas." While meditation was great in theory it often proved impossibly difficult to sustain in practice.

Then in the 1980s a very important shift started to happen. Western professionals who had been drawn to meditation, often out of a deep intellectual curiosity, began to write about their experiences for a more middle-class Western audience. Herbert Benson, Ainslie Meares, Joan Borysenko, Laurence Le Shan, Ian Gawler, Jon Kabat-Zinn, to name a few, started writing about meditation in a secular context, as a practice that could be used particularly for health and well-being. The key insight they presented, each in their own unique style, was the focus on conscious deep relaxation as a gateway to meditation.

My own experience when I encountered this particular focus for meditation is important to relate here. In 1991, I started working as a therapist with Dr. Ian Gawler at his rural residential center at Yarra Junction on the outskirts of Melbourne. The center provides regular ten-day live-in self-help programs for cancer patients and their families. Ian Gawler's remarkable recovery from widely disseminated metastatic bone cancer is detailed in his book *You Can Conquer Cancer*.[2] He attributes his healing principally to his passionate espousal of positive thinking, healthy diet and meditation. He had been taught to meditate by the Melbourne psychiatrist Dr. Ainslie Meares in 1975 when his cancer was widespread and not responding to any conventional treatments. After he got well, Ian Gawler went on to teach a form of meditation derived from Dr. Meares' technique.[3]

I started working with Ian Gawler primarily because of my credentials as a keen meditator for the previous fifteen years. It was a whole new learning for me. Both Ian Gawler and Ainslie Meares

emphasized physical *relaxation* rather than religious or spiritual outcomes. (I later learned that both these men assumed that if their
clients persevered with their meditation practice they would frequently have spiritual experiences.)

In my meditation practice prior to this time no great focus had
been given to the body or the idea of taking time gently and consciously to relax the body. Buddhism is primarily about the mind:
all of the instructions I had received to that time focused on the
training of the mind. Detailed instructions had, of course, been
given on posture; I struggled endlessly to have good meditative posture. In retrospect, my response to the instructions was rather mil-
itaristic, even hostile, in my attitude toward my body. The body had
to be subdued, made pliant and compliant. In 1991, I experienced
what was to me a startling revelation at that time: all those years I
had been trying so hard in my meditation practice, but my body
was so stiff, so tense, so overwrought through all that effort.
Buddhist teachings give a strong focus to the mind-body connection, but I realized I was focusing wholly on the mind at the
expense of the body. In my work with Ian Gawler all this changed.

I started regularly practising simple deep relaxation techniques.
The result was immediate and enormously surprising: my meditation effortlessly deepened and I was able to sustain it session after
session. It dawned on me then that for all the years I'd been passionately working on my mind I had also unwittingly been at war
with my body. What's more, I started meeting cancer patients who
were doing this simple relaxation-based meditation, often for many
hours a day, and achieving remarkable, unexpected remissions,
heightened feelings of well-being and occasionally complete healing
recoveries.

A further goal of this book then is to help aspiring meditation
students to avoid this pitfall—and perhaps to help others lighten up
in their practice! One of the saddest comments I repeatedly heard
in my years of teaching meditation is a sense of failure about the
practice: "I know meditation is important but I never do enough"
or some variation on this theme. For so many practitioners their
meditation becomes a chore, something they should be doing more

of, something they're endlessly failing at. In the groups I've led over the years I've emphasized that people give time to work lovingly and kindly with the body, giving a high priority to deep, simple relaxation. This works as an antidote to the feeling of endless struggle, while reinforcing an effortless ease with, and confidence in, our daily practice.

Before describing the practice in detail, I want to summarize why this emphasis on physical relaxation as the gateway into the practice can be so helpful. In the 1970s, Ainslie Meares presented a simple thesis to his cancer patients: *your body knows how to heal.* He told them to practice getting out of the way; let their body and mind come back to a state of simple balance and harmony and then rest in that state as long as they can.[4] The body's ability to heal is fundamental to our being. Through a lifetime experience of compromise, disappointment, failure, fear, stress, grief and loss we often lose connectedness with this deeply instinctual healing ability. The effectiveness of the body's healing system can become blunted, the immune system distracted by the deeply ingrained habits of worry and anxiety, the body constantly drenched in stress hormones, further weakening the vigilance of the immune system. Dr. Meares argued that through the deep conscious relaxation of meditation there is less anxiety, worry and fear; less adrenaline and cortisol; and the body is freer to heal. This simple and elegant thesis has inspired cancer patients for over twenty-five years. It is a practice that offers rich rewards for everyone. We shouldn't be so blithely unaware that it requires a life-threatening illness to push us to make a start.

THE PRACTICE OF RELAXATION

The practice is simple. There are a number of techniques that all have the same intent: to give the practitioner a strategy for slowly and intentionally relaxing all the major muscle groupings in the body. The goal is to enable the practitioner to experience the whole body as relaxed. This experience deepens steadily over time with diligent practice.

There are two essential keys to this simple practice. The first is to do it slowly, step by step, again and again. Gently and persistently familiarize the body with what it feels like to be relaxed in every muscle group. It is a slow, conscious re-education of the body. Most of us tend to think we are relaxed when we are not; we have become used to having tension permanently fixed in many places in the body. More often than not we are unaware of how tense and contracted we are. I have encountered many people over the years whose bodies have almost set like concrete from decades of unrelieved worry and anxiety. They are frequently aware of their extreme levels of tension but feel utterly defeated by any efforts they make to relax and unwind. Often these people have said to me in the early weeks of their meditation, with a resigned shrug of the shoulders, "Well, that's just how I am." The good news is that this can be changed: just like our mind, our body is potentially quite malleable and very appreciative of kindness, care, and nurturance. I love the Old Testament saying that the body is the temple of the soul. One of my friends often says, as he goes off to his meditation room, "I'm just going off to care for the temple for a while."

The process of re-educating the body generally takes many months, even years, so deeply ingrained are our habits of holding and resistance. At the start there is often a "whoosh of well-being." This experience comes from simply taking time to be with the body in a loving and attentive way. It is common to have these "honeymoon" experiences when we first start to meditate: the body and mind instantly recognize and delight in the new experience of relaxation and letting go. However, our old ways don't go that easily: it is difficult to change a life-long habit of storing all our pain and sorrow and stress in our body. On a scale of zero to ten, where zero equals deeply relaxed and ten equals our normal level of tension, it is relatively easy to bring the level down to five or four; but the remaining points on the scale require diligent attentive practice, generally over quite a long period of time. Another factor that commonly undermines the continuing effectiveness of this practice is familiarity. After a period of time it is quite easy to go on automatic—"Oh, I know how to do this now"—then become distracted and inattentive.

The second key to the practice of relaxation is to focus on the feelings in the body. Most of the techniques detailed in later chapters of this book require an ability to focus on a specific object of attention, for example, the breath, a mantra, an idea or an image. Not so with relaxation: The instruction is, "When the mind wanders, as soon as you notice, come back to that place in your body and the feelings you notice." This attention to feelings in the body becomes finer and more acute as the practice deepens. From session to session, you start to notice with increasing sensitivity fine differences of feeling in different parts of the body. In this way the practice is always new, always fresh. Each session there are different levels and degrees of sensation and location in the body. This is a wonderful antidote to boredom or laziness in the practice.

Many methods of meditation use a relaxation technique as the gateway into the quiet stillness that is needed for the practice. None of them require you to master an elaborate technique. There is no complex philosophy or belief system involved. In fact, relaxation is something you can do at your own pace and in your own way; hence it is categorically not something that you can get wrong or fail at.

Another factor that most of the relaxation techniques have in common is the instruction to begin the focus of attention with the feet and work slowly up through the body to finish at the crown of the head or the forehead. In this way, the physical feelings of ease and letting go are gently moved up through the body and into the mind. Most meditation techniques require the practitioner to maintain a rigorous attention to a strategy designed to train the mind, generally after a brief period for settling the body. But here the focus on the body is used as a way of showing the mind how to become quiet and relax and let go. It is as if the relaxation slowly ripples up through the body and into the mind without excessive effort or force: your focus is on the feelings in the body, step by step.

It is worth lingering on the "feeling focus" of relaxation strategies a little longer. The feeling that helps to deepen the practice is the feeling of "letting go." The phrase "letting go" has for some time been in danger of becoming a cliché; yet there is no more simple or eloquent an expression that could be used. It so aptly describes your goal. In the progressive muscle relaxation technique you tightly contract the muscles then release them to give you a direct physical experience of letting go. In the autogenic and body-scan techniques (described in the next chapter) you experience the letting-go feeling more subtly: with the breath or simply through the gentle focus of attention on specific parts of the body. For nearly all of us the lifetime habit has been one of "holding on": to tension and stress in the body; to resentment, fear, anger and other powerful emotions; to "me and mine"; to our attitudes; to our views of right and wrong, good and bad; to our likes and dislikes. One primary goal of meditation is to become more aware of these rigid, ingrained habits of holding on, then softening them with a more open, gentle, non-judging stance. For most of us this is the work of a lifetime.

When the focus is on letting go, the simplest place to start is the body. The mental and emotional holding-on is so much more subtle, ingrained and unconscious. It is common at the beginning to experience very quickly extensive and deep levels of physical letting-go: the muscle fibers loosening and lengthening, the breath softening and deepening, the body feeling heavier. A consequence of this letting-go at the physical level is that the mind and emotions also begin to benefit from a flow-on experience of the softening, relaxing and releasing. The richness of this approach is that it can be done without force or striving: there are no compulsory experiences. The practitioner is simply invited to rest in the physical sensations of the body with a quiet, gentle, open-minded curiosity. The experience is often likened to a gentle, rippling, upwards flow of the relaxation feelings from the lower half of the body, through the trunk, the arms and shoulders, the neck, face and scalp and, without any seeming effort, into the mind.

In his pioneering book *The Relaxation Response*, Dr. Herbert Benson argued that the relaxation response is the body's natural experience at the completion of the cycle of instantaneous arousal of the fight-or-flight response, which is hard-wired into our bodies.[5] Our problem is that we rarely get to this state of completion after the arousal. There are two fundamental reasons for this. Firstly, because the holding-on pattern is so entrenched in us by habit, and secondly, because so many of the crises and stresses of modern life never reach a resolution. What we can do is train ourselves to cultivate deliberately and consciously the experience of the relaxation response. As we familiarize ourselves with this state in regular daily meditation, it becomes easier to access the relaxation response within the periods of meditation practice and later in the ups and downs of daily living. The repeated experience of deep relaxation in regular meditation practice becomes a new way of responding to events, and being in our body, that automatically flows into daily living.

New meditation practitioners often complain to me that they are not "getting it," nothing much is happening in their practice. By this they generally mean that they are bored or still have the "monkey-mind" or that they are not having the type of experience they have read or heard about. But when I question them about what is happening in their life, they often say they are sleeping better or are less reactive to all the things that used to disturb them so easily. Even better, they may comment that their spouse or children or friends have been commenting about how much nicer they are or how much easier to live with. These kinds of outcomes are generally the first major benefit of the deep relaxation focus as an approach to meditation. And, just as frequently, these outcomes are diminished or overlooked as the meditator longs for one of the amazing experiences they expect.

Earlier in this book, I explained why slow, conscious, deep relaxation can be a skillful gateway into meditation: as you focus on relaxing the body, your mind becomes calmer without any extra effort on your part. The trick is to remember to do it! It is a meditation technique that requires time and diligence. There is nothing magical about it; in fact it can sometimes feel mechanical. In essence it is a slow re-education of the body, with a marvelous and often unexpected follow-on effect in the mind. In the next chapter some of the most frequently used relaxation techniques are described, with meditation exercises for practical application. Experiment with them to find those that suit you best.

chapter 5

Relaxation Techniques

It is not uncommon for me to meet people who disparage relaxation techniques as kindergarten practices suitable only for beginners. Not only is this an arrogant and wrong-headed view, but my experience sitting in meditation with some of the people who make such comments is that they often seem fidgety and restless. Even worse, sometimes it seems like they are operating on automatic, deeply bored with the "higher" forms of practice they might be doing.

A primary goal of relaxation techniques, and of the mindfulness tradition that is the focus of chapters six and seven, is to have an in-the-body experience. The aim is to be *here*, present and on the spot. To achieve that we need to be fully present in our body, not lost in mental abstraction, fantasy or memory, which is our usual habit. While relaxation is a skillful, ongoing focus for an experienced meditator at the commencement of every session, and a wise starting point for a new meditator, it is *essential* for those coming to meditation for healing, whether it be physical, emotional, mental or spiritual.

Most schools of physical yoga end a session with a few minutes of relaxation. For many of us this is our first experience of what it feels like to be really relaxed and at peace. When relaxation is used as a gateway into meditation it is the focus of the practice. Initially the slow, detailed attention to the step-by-step process of physical relaxation takes up most of the allotted time, with only a brief period spent in the non-doing time of quiet stillness. As you become accustomed to the process and familiar with the experience of relaxation, the time spent in relaxation can be progressively shortened, leaving increasing periods of time for meditation. You can then go on to other forms of practice confident in your ability to sit in a deeply relaxed state with a consciously cultivated and genuine feeling of balance and harmony in body and mind. This is a wonderful platform from which to move on to more demanding practices, most of which involve the cultivation of a single-pointed concentration on an object of attention.

For some, the deep relaxation experience is enough. You may have no interest in going any deeper with your practice; perhaps you are not especially interested in spiritual outcomes, or you may be focused on a particular goal and feel you only need the relaxation process. I have worked with many people who have tried a range of meditation techniques but returned to a deep, slow relaxation method as their meditation of choice because it gives them access to the experiences they seek.

Experienced meditators who have mastered the relaxation process find it helpful to return regularly to this practice to experience the sheer delight of the slow, attentive relaxation experience. I strongly recommend this as it is a simple way to maintain a connection with the experience of deep ease and well-being, which is the most reliable base for the sustained long-term practice of meditation.

Most people prefer to do the relaxation techniques lying down. There is a possibility that you will fall asleep, so be aware of your state of mind and level of fatigue. These techniques also work well in a sitting position or the more traditional cross-legged or kneeling postures. The focus is on the actual relaxation experience in a slow, step-by-step manner. Initially the relaxation process itself occupies most of the time, with a short period of quiet stillness at the end. Some of the techniques, for example the autogenic training, begin with only a few minutes of practice; others such as the body scan can last for up to forty minutes. If you are a beginner you need to be aware of the time frame best for you. You do not have to be rigid about it. On busy days, choose an abbreviated technique. When you have more time, use one of the more extensive and leisurely techniques.

LONGER RELAXATION TECHNIQUES

AUTOGENIC TRAINING

This technique has been used extensively in hospitals, universities and a wide variety of other clinical settings. It is one of the first deliberate uses of a deep relaxation technique in the West. The essence of this practice is the use of words as a form of "autosuggestion" that the meditator slowly repeats, suggesting warmth and heaviness in the limbs. There is a sequence of standard exercises that are aimed at reversing the stored arousal left in the body from our chronic inability to complete the fight-or-flight response. This sequence can be built up over a number of weeks.

Following is a progression of instructions you can follow regularly for a few minutes a day, over a course of a couple of months. In the first few weeks the theme of heaviness in the muscles is built. You are invited to recite verbal formulae such as "My right arm is heavy; my left arm is heavy; both of my arms are heavy." These phrases are then successively increased to include the legs. After a few weeks this is simplified to the statement, "My arms and legs are heavy." You are encouraged to pause for a few minutes regularly throughout the day and repeat these simple phrases.

After a few weeks focusing on the theme of heaviness, add other words on the theme of warmth. The aim is to assist in increasing peripheral blood flow in the arms and legs in order to reverse the pooling of blood in the trunk and head that is a feature of the fight-or-flight response. Examples of the words used are: "My right arm is warm; my left arm is warm; both my arms are warm." Again, these phrases are repeated for a week or so then the legs are added: "My right leg is warm; my left leg is warm; both of my legs are warm." After another week the themes of warmth and heaviness are combined and added to the above: "My arms and legs are heavy; my arms and legs are warm; my arms and legs are heavy and warm."

Further themes designed to deepen the relaxation of the body are slowly added. The focus of these is to normalize cardiac activity, regulate the respiratory system, relax and warm the abdominal region and reduce the flow of blood to the head. Examples of the phrases used in these additional exercises are, "My heartbeat is calm and regular; it breathes me; my solar plexus is warm; my forehead is cool."

When you have mastered these standard exercises of autogenic training, usually over a few months, you can develop your own words or themes to deal with specific problems. Some examples might be, "My shoulders are soft and relaxed; my hands are warm; my throat is relaxed and my breathing is easy; my breath comes effortlessly into my body, it is calm and relaxed." Once you have learned to relax deeply by focusing on these simple physical functions, you will be able to spend more time in meditation free from distraction and restlessness.

PROGRESSIVE MUSCLE RELAXATION

This technique has also been used widely in clinical settings. In my experience it is a powerful technique that can flow into a deep experience of peace and well-being.

Begin with your attention at the feet and focus the attention progressively up through the body on each major muscle group in turn. Focus on the feeling sensations in the muscles, which are slowly contracted then slowly relaxed. As in most relaxation strategies it is important to slow the process down, to train yourself to become more deeply attentive to what you feel.

To facilitate the slow, attentive pace of this technique, try to observe each muscle group at four different levels of experience:

- Firstly, observe how the feet feel when you begin. Notice whether they are warm or cold, how they contact with socks or carpet or shoes, even how the toes feel when you wriggle them a little.

- Secondly, notice the feeling of tension or tightness when you contract the muscles.
- Thirdly, notice the feeling of releasing and letting go when you relax the contraction.
- Finally, observe the feelings of softness, ease and relaxation in the muscles when you complete the letting go.

At all four levels you will over time develop an awareness of increasingly subtle levels of feeling brought about by this slow, detailed training of attention to observe finer degrees of sensation in the muscles.

There is great benefit to be gained from the physical contracting and releasing in this technique. It is one of the most effective ways of taking the body through all the major muscle groups, giving attention to the experience of softening, releasing and relaxing in each group of muscles. This technique invites you to delight in the feelings of ease and well-being in each muscle grouping before moving on to the next group. It is also an excellent tool for training awareness, which is pivotal to all other meditation techniques.

The major muscle groups focused on are, in order:

- the feet and ankles
- the calves; the thighs
- the buttocks and pelvic area
- the belly and lower back
- the chest and upper back
- the arms and hands
- the shoulders and neck
- the jaw, face, and eyes
- the scalp
- the forehead

By finishing at the forehead you indirectly invite the mind to join with the process. People using this method frequently report an effortless flowing into the mind of the feelings of softening, releasing, relaxing and letting go that have been slowly experienced physically in the body.

This technique can initially be a problem for very tense people. The process of contracting can lock an even greater level of tension into the muscles with no concomitant feeling for how to let go. If this is your experience I encourage you to focus on the muscles without the process of contraction and to just imagine letting go (or even just the *possibility* of letting go). After a time you should be able to move on to the physical contracting and letting go. The great advantage of this technique of physically contracting and releasing is that it shows the body how to do it muscle group after muscle group. It is almost like saying to your body, "This is how it feels when you are tight and tense, and this is how it feels when you have let go and are relaxed." It is a slow but very powerful re-education of the body and mind.

THE BODY SCAN

This is a subtler and generally more drawn-out method of relaxation. After settling into a comfortable posture, noticing sounds and sensations with an attitude of passive observation, you are invited to cultivate a focus on the movement of the breath for a few minutes. After these preliminaries, the focus of physical relaxation begins at the feet. Attention is first directed to one foot. The goal is then to slowly bring your full awareness to the toes, one by one, then the various planes and surfaces of the foot, the joints, tendons, ligaments, the ankle, the heel, the sole. The focusing of attention is done in slow, minute detail, combined with breath awareness. As you slowly focus on each part of the foot you are encouraged to imagine bringing the in-breath down through the whole body to that part of the foot, and breathing out again from that part, up through the body and out through the nostrils.

In this technique you move attention slowly from the foot to the ankle, then to the shin, the calf, the knee and the thigh. Then you redirect attention to the other leg, starting at the toes again. As the description implies, this detailed scanning process moves slowly and progressively up through the whole body, focusing in detail on as many aspects of bodily awareness as possible. Unlike the progressive muscle relaxation technique, it is not limited just to feelings in the muscles; and it is more passive, without the focus on contracting and relaxing.

Many people tell me that they find this technique particularly helps them to go deeper because of the focus on joints and skin texture as well as the muscles, and also because of the more minute attention to small, detailed parts of the body. For example, when scanning the knee, you are invited to observe the kneecap, the flat sides of the knee, and the softer, sticky skin at the back of the knee; to simply be aware of all the work this complex joint does throughout the day. You then deepen the attention into the cartilage and tendons that hold the knee together.

The body scan proceeds up through the hip joints, the buttocks, the sexual organs, the lower back, the belly (involving an awareness of all the organs and viscera of the abdomen), the middle and upper back, the shoulder blades and the chest (including the lungs and heart inside the protective shield of the ribcage). It moves to the individual fingers, hands, wrists, forearms, elbows, and upper arm of each arm, one at a time. Then it moves to the shoulders, neck, throat (including an awareness of the esophagus, trachea, blood vessels and cervical vertebrae), face, mouth, tongue, nose, cheeks, eyes, temples, ears, scalp, forehead and crown of the head.

A lovely way of ending this practice was developed by Jon Kabat-Zinn.[1] When finishing the body scan at the crown of the head: imagine breathing in through the crown of the head and out through the soles of the feet, then reverse it with the next breath to imagine breathing in through the soles of the feet and out through the crown of the head. Imagine the tumbling flow of the breath down through the whole body then up through the whole body. Maintain this pattern for a while, experiencing yourself as a whole organism, at one with the breath. You can rest in this pattern for a while then slowly let go of the image; just rest in the feeling of well-being, breath by breath.

For many people, the body-scan experience can be like a deep, often surprising and emotional homecoming. For the first time they can feel deeply connected to the whole body, releasing a flood of emotion, relief, well-being and, sometimes, tears. For many years I have found a combination of the body scan and progressive muscle relaxation techniques very helpful in introducing people to an effective relaxation experience. The guided meditation for this method is on page 59.

AINSLIE MEARES' STILLNESS METHOD

Ainslie Meares was an Australian psychiatrist who was often described as "a doctor ahead of his time."[2] In the 1980s he was a leading world authority on the use of clinical hypnosis to help patients with serious medical and psychiatric conditions. He travelled widely and on one of his trips was introduced to a yogi in Kathmandu who taught him to meditate. The experience was so profound for him that he returned home to Melbourne and started teaching meditation to his patients. This interest grew to the point that meditation became almost the sole focus of his practice. He wrote many books outlining his ideas and method of practice. He was very influential during his life and his influence continues to grow after his death. He was generally misunderstood and often pilloried by his peers in the medical profession for his passionate interest in and promotion of meditation.

Ainslie Meares had his own unique understanding of meditation and deep, simple relaxation was crucial to the practice he taught. He gave considerable thought to how to integrate meditation into a Western understanding. His books, written before the widespread appearance of Eastern ideas in the West, are still insightful and unique in their lack of mysticism. The Meares technique is highly idiosyncratic and is quite dependent on the presence of the meditation teacher. Meares developed his own language and phrasing, together with quite intimate personal touch, as the method for taking participants into deep states of relaxation and meditation.

For Meares, the meditative experience was best characterized as an experience of simple stillness. He coined a term for this experience: *mental ataraxis*. Meares led participants into a deep state of relaxation and letting go by a mix of three ingredients. Firstly, he used very general phrases to encourage deep relaxation: "letting go," "feeling it all through," "you don't have to do anything," "simply letting go," "more and more," "deeper and deeper." Secondly, he used gentle, lingering physical touch on the shoulders, chest, back, arms and abdomen. Thirdly, he deliberately used garbled phrases and expressions, even grunts and mumbled non-words, to scramble logical thinking.

The Meares method is about creating a pathway to enable us to rest in a state of non-doing, so that our body and mind can rest together in an experience of harmony and balance—or stillness, to use Meares' preferred word. In this state, he argued, we are more able to cultivate a connection to good health and calm well-being. In his time it proved remarkably effective and he documented many examples of healing and unexpected remission among his patients with advanced disease. There are a few teachers in Australia still promoting and teaching the Meares method.

Ainslie Meares stands as an interesting example of the early stirrings of interest in meditation in Australia. His most powerful attribute was that he trusted his own deep experiences in meditation, and he taught and wrote directly from those experiences. He also wrote simple and eloquent poetry about his experiences in meditation.

RAPID RELAXATION TECHNIQUES

There are a number of ways that you can shorten the relaxation process so you can spend more time in quiet meditation. This is particularly relevant once you have confidently learnt how to practice and then deepen the experience of physical relaxation through the whole body, and felt its flow-on effect into the mind.

FOCUSING ON THE BREATH

At the beginning of a session it is helpful to take a number of deep, full inhalations through the nostrils, breathing out through the mouth. With practice the out-breath becomes a reminder of the experience of letting go, cueing the whole body back into the remembered experience of deep relaxation. It is also helpful to add an audible sigh with the out-breath; repeat that deep, sighing out-breath as many times as you find helpful in the first few minutes of your meditation time.

Taking a sequence of deep, full breaths like this draws feelings of physical tightness and tension into the chest and then allows them to be sighed away on the out-breath through the mouth. When you are confident with this method, three or four deep breaths will be enough to trigger the relaxation response. However, when you start you will probably get more benefit from eight or more of these deep breaths. When you finish the sequence of deep breaths let your breath return to its normal easy pattern, breathing in and out through the nostrils if you can do so comfortably. This simple technique works very well once you are familiar with what it feels like to be deeply relaxed. The deep sighs are like a bodily cue to drop effortlessly into the letting go of deep relaxation.

USING A WORD OR PHRASE

At the commencement of a session, a simple word or phrase, generally combined with the out-breath, can be very helpful. Some examples are: relaxing, releasing, letting go, calm, effortlessly, all through, I don't have to do anything. Some people find it more helpful to have a different word for the in-breaths and out-breaths: for example, peace (in-breath), love (out-breath). A combination I have found very helpful, especially for times of sickness or trouble, is: renewing (in-breath), releasing (out-breath). You may find it more beneficial to use a word or a phrase that feels special to you. A person with a religious outlook might find it helpful to say a short repetitive prayer or mantra.

FOCUSING ON YOUR OWN BODILY TENSION POINT

Most of us are familiar with a particular point in the body where we hold our tension and stress. There are some places in the body that are common to most people, for example, the shoulders, the belly, the jaw, the forehead and the lower back. Over the years I have noticed that people can have quite personal, even idiosyncratic, tension points. Some examples are the sternum, the soles of the feet, the hands, the eyes or the temples. If you are not sure where this spot is for you, pay careful attention to your body; over time you will learn where it is. You may have a few of these tension points in your body.

Once you are familiar with the experience of deep relaxation, focusing on relaxing and softening this personal tension point can be enough to precipitate a cascading experience of relaxation throughout the body.

USING SMALL, SPECIFIC MOVEMENTS

A practice I have found particularly helpful to precipitate rapid relaxation is to use some small, specific and consciously sloweddown movements of the body. Some examples are flexing the hip joints, moving the shoulders up and down, moving the hands and fingers, swaying the back from side to side, swaying the head, and stretching the spine by gently lifting up at the crown of the head. Slowly swaying the head can be particularly helpful for sitting meditation if you have problems with stiffness or soreness in the neck when sitting for long periods. Swaying the head at the beginning of every meditation session helps to loosen the muscles in your neck and throat; it also helps you to find a balanced position for the head. If you like to meditate lying down you can get a similar benefit by gently rolling the head from side to side.

SELF-HYPNOSIS

There is a large literature on self-hypnosis techniques for the layperson. As opposed to Buddhist meditation, in self-hypnosis focus is more on working with the subconscious mind by using some repetitive trance-inducing phrases, or strategies like counting to take yourself into a light trance. In the trance state you then repeat words and phrases that reinforce your intended goal. Many people find these techniques very helpful, but I believe you can get more sustained benefit from the focus on alert intentionality in the traditional practices of meditation.

USING MUSIC

Music is very widely used as a support to meditation, especially by people who want to have some "time-out" aided by gently ambient background music. There is a wide range of music specially recorded for this purpose, some of it incorporating natural sounds. There is also a choice between stand-alone recorded music and guided meditations with music in the background.

Because of my long involvement in the Buddhist meditation tradition, I have rarely meditated with music. My training has also made me resistant to the idea of meditation as entertainment, or the desire to gently "sugar the pill." However, over the years many people have told me that they always have their best meditation experiences with gentle background music. So if music works for you, use it. Having said that, I would still like to encourage you to experiment by alternating practicing with silence; I also encourage you to allow yourself to be patient and curious about the possibilities afforded by simple silence. The French philosopher Blaise Pascal eloquently reminds us of the value of this: he wrote that all of mankind's problems are caused by our inability to sit quietly in a room by ourselves alone.[3]

We all tend to be creatures of habit. Those who start with music often find it hard to move away from this background stimulus; I have a bias toward silence and stillness. There is a challenging paradox at work here. When you start your meditation practice it is helpful to find a method, a technique, a teacher and a lineage that speaks to you; then to commit to a regular, disciplined practice that feels appropriate. However, as you become more confident and established in your meditation practice, you also need to keep your questioning and critical faculties alive. Don't stay in a tradition or practice because it feels safe or comfortable. The Buddha warned against this kind of uncritical complacency.

One of my early teachers, a charismatic Tibetan Buddhist monk in exile called Lama Yeshe, would always challenge his students, "You check up, dear, check up whether this is true or not." I invite you—challenge you—to review and assess regularly whether your meditation practice is useful and helpful in your life. The following chapters introduce meditation practices to help you deepen your experience and continue to cultivate this commitment to "checking up."

EXERCISE

GUIDED RELAXATION MEDITATION

This meditation has been written as a guided practice. It is helpful to record it for yourself, or ask a friend to do it for you. Remember, the pacing needs to be slower than normal speech, and you need to pause between sentences. Be aware that your tone of voice is very important in setting the mood. With practice you will become more skilled. It is helpful to hear how experienced teachers lead a meditation session. Set aside at least half an hour to do this meditation.

Take time to make sure you can sit or lie comfortably in the posture you have chosen for the next half-hour or more. Then take a few moments to make any small adjustments to help yourself feel more comfortable. Check in with your body. Notice how it feels. Let the weight of your body soften a little more, releasing down into those places of contact and pressure, releasing down into the gentle pull of gravity. No force, just feeling your presence, right here, on the spot.

Now take a few moments to clear your mind and establish your focus, your motivation. You might like to silently say to yourself in your mind: "This is a time for healing, a time I give to myself for my healing. I want my life to be meaningful and purposeful. The greatest meaning for my life is to be able to help others. This is my meaning and purpose, and to be able to achieve this purpose I need a healthy body and a calm mind. For that reason I am going to do this practice, so that I can more skillfully help others as well as myself."

Now, when you are ready, take three or four deep, full breaths, in through the nostrils and out through the mouth. You may like to make an audible sigh with the out-breath. Release fully and completely with each out-breath. Then let your breath return to its own easy natural rhythm, breathing through the nostrils if you can. Rest your attention on the flowing movement of each breath for a while now. (In a recording, leave thirty seconds of silence here.)

Now take your attention down into your feet. Notice how your feet are feeling today. Remember that for this practice the focus is on the feelings in your body. Notice as much as you can about your feet and ankles. Now take a few moments to gently move your toes and your feet. Make the movements conscious and slow. Then, with an out-breath, let go of the movements and feel your feet and ankles softening and relaxing with the letting go, flowing down into the support of the floor, soft and easy and relaxed all through, the feet feeling soft and relaxed, soft and relaxed.

Then, gently move your attention up into your calves. Notice how they are feeling, or any contact with clothing or the floor. Now, with your attention fully on the calves, flex and release them a few times. Flex and release, feeling it in the knees as well. As you let go that flexing and releasing feel the letting go, soft and relaxed all through the calves, soft and relaxed.

Now bring your attention up into your thighs, noticing any contact with the floor or the chair. These are the longest muscles in your body. Notice how they feel, notice contact with clothing. Then gently flex and release your thigh muscles a few times, attending to the feeling of flexing and releasing. Now let the thigh muscles release, on an out-breath, for the last time, the muscles releasing completely and effortlessly into the support of the chair or the floor, soft and relaxed, soft and relaxed. Feel it all through the legs now. The legs might even feel a little heavier. Feel the letting go and simply go with it, flowing with it, all through the legs.

Next move your attention into the hips and buttocks, the whole of your pelvic area. Feel how the weight of the body flows down through the buttocks into the floor or the chair. Notice as well the contact with clothing. Now gently and slowly begin to flex and release both hip joints, feeling the movement in the hips and buttocks and all through the pelvic area. Then on an out-breath complete the final release. Feel the weight of the body flowing down into the floor or chair more completely now, releasing, relaxing and letting go, all through the hips and buttocks. Sometimes it can feel like the whole pelvic girdle has softened and opened a little. Feel the letting go and simply go with it, flowing with it, easy and relaxed all through the lower half of the body now. Effortlessly now, going with it, flowing with it.

Now move your attention to your belly and your lower back. Notice how your belly feels. Notice any constriction from elastic or a belt around the tummy, notice contact with clothing. Feel how your belly gently rises and falls with your breath. Notice how that rising and falling of your breath flows into the muscles of the lower back as well. Be present to all the feelings in your belly and lower back, be aware of the organs and viscera of your body inside the belly, rising and falling. Now see if you can allow your belly to soften some more. You don't need to hold the belly tight or hard any more. Let it go, letting the belly fall forward some more, softening more and more through the belly. Feel that letting go in the lower back as well. Flow with it, soft and relaxed in the belly and in the lower back. Feel the breath effortlessly flowing in the rising and falling of the belly, easy and relaxed, easy and relaxed.

Next, move your attention to the spine and the back. If you are lying down, feel how the bony ridge of the spine is in contact with the floor. If you are sitting, feel the erect upthrust of the spine. Feel the subtle movements in the back as it flexes with each breath, the shoulder blades rising and falling with each breath. Now introduce some small, gentle movements into the back. If you are sitting, sway slowly from side to side, across the point of balance, with the base of the spine as the fulcrum. If you are lying down, roll a little from side to side across the bony ridge of the spine, small, gentle movements, the vertebrae finding their own easy, natural alignment. Then, on an out-breath, bring that movement to an end, letting the back rest effortlessly now, balanced and relaxed, all through, up and down the length of the back, easy and relaxed.

Next, let your attention come to your chest. Feel the rising and falling of the ribs, the movement of the life-breath in your body. Feel the strength of your rib-cage, the effortless rhythm of the breath and the heart-beat in your body. These great natural rhythms of your body, rising and falling. Now, take a sequence of slow, deep breaths. Feel the fullness of these breaths. Feel how the lungs inside the body push out against the rib-cage and down into the diaphragm. (In a recording, leave thirty seconds of silence.) Now, after releasing the final deep breath, allow your breathing to return to its own natural rhythm. Once again, feel the simple rhythm of the breath, the life-breath. Let the breath breathe you, effortlessly now, the breath that's breathing you, flow with it, simply flowing with it.

Now bring your awareness into your arms and hands. Notice any contact of your arms and hands with the rest of your body or the floor. Notice the sensitivity in your hands and fingers. Be aware of how their weight flows down into those places of contact and pressure. Now take some time to slowly move your arms and hands, the fingers, the wrist and the elbows; gentle, slow movements with full awareness. Then, when you are ready, let go of those movements on an exhalation. Allow the arms and hands to rest where they are, soft and relaxed, all through the arms and hands, soft and relaxed. You may experience the hands feeling different in some way as they soften and relax even more.

Now move your awareness up into your shoulders. Feel the set of your shoulders. So often we store our worries and tensions in our shoulders, the burdens we carry. Be present to your shoulders however they feel today. Feel the weight of the arms hanging down off the shoulders. Now, start to gently move your shoulders, lifting them up and letting them drop, very slowly. Move them in a gentle front-to-back movement a few times, each small movement softening through the shoulders. Then with a slow, deep exhalation let go of all the movement. Let the shoulders drop a little more, dropping some more, soft and easy and relaxed all through the shoulders now, all through, feel it all through the body, easy and relaxed, feeling the letting go and going with it.

Next bring your attention to your neck and throat, all the muscles and blood vessels, and the cervical spine, the esophagus and trachea, connecting the head and the body. Sometimes there is stiffness or soreness in the neck. Become more aware of your neck and throat. Now begin to slowly move your head. If you are lying, roll the head very slowly from side to side. If you are sitting, slowly sway the head from side to side and front to back. You can also turn the head a little, keeping all the movements slow and conscious. If you are sitting, feel for that point of balance as the head moves through it. (Allow enough time for the movements.) Now begin to slow down and lessen the movements. Bring the head to rest. If you are sitting, make sure your head is resting in that point of balance, resting effortlessly in that point of balance.

Now bring your awareness into your face. Feel the hinge of the jaw below your ears, the point of your jaw, how your lips are touching. Notice the feeling of the skin across your cheeks and temples, how your eyelids are touching. Be aware of the myriad tiny muscles in the face that constantly register emotions, thoughts, feelings and reactions. Now take a few moments to slowly move the jaw. In those movements soften the mouth as well, the lips sliding against each other slightly. Then, when you are ready, let go of the movements of the jaw. Let the jaw drop a little so that the lips are lightly touching. Allow all the muscles through the face to soften and lengthen and relax, through the cheeks, around the eyes, the nostrils, soft and relaxed. In the corners of the mouth, across the temples, the eyelids lightly touching, feel the letting go all through the face now, flowing with it, up through the back of the head, the scalp and the crown of the head, soft and relaxed all through the scalp. Then lastly allow the forehead to become softer and smoother, all the muscles across the forehead and through the eyebrows, long and soft and relaxed.

Feel it all through the body now, easy and relaxed. Simply rest in it now, relaxed in the body and in the mind, feeling it all through, relaxing and letting go. You don't have to do anything. Resting in it now, all through, effortlessly, calm and relaxed.

(You may find it helpful to add the following optional instruction to focus on the breathing for a while.)

Now gently bring your awareness to rest again on the rhythm of the breath. Feel again this deep, life-long rhythm of your body, renewing on the in-breath and releasing on the out-breath, staying with that simple, effortless movement of the breath, renewing and releasing. If your mind wanders, as soon as you notice gently bring your attention back to the breath, renewing and releasing. (In a recording, leave as much time in silence as you would like.)

Now, in a moment it will be time to bring this meditation to an end. Being aware of your breathing again, start to take some deeper, fuller breaths now, and as you breathe out, gently move first your feet and your legs, then your arms and hands. Move the back, breathing deeply into the belly now. Move your head gently. Before you open your eyes, just rest for a few moments, aware of how your body feels and the state of your mind. You may like to end the meditation with a simple dedication: "As a result of this meditation, may I be happy and well and may my practice be a cause to bring healing and well-being to all."

The purpose of the above meditation is to give you a structure for a detailed relaxation technique so that you can practice it to gain confidence to guide yourself and others. When you have used it a few times you can begin to add phrases and language that may feel more helpful to you, and also delete phrases and sections that don't feel helpful. The script is a starting point (often in an abbreviated form) for many of the meditations in later chapters. In subsequent meditation techniques it is assumed that you are familiar with the process and experience of relaxation.

chapter 6

Mindfulness: Creating a Non-choosing Awareness

Mindfulness meditation is about coming into a relationship with ourselves and the world as they actually are rather than how we would like them to be. In our meditation practice this is expressed as a willingness to work with whatever is, whatever presents itself. All the experiences of our life are brought into the meditation and there is no attempt to alter or change them in any way. In this type of meditation practice there is no seeking after another state of being, no attempt to superimpose an elevated image or to distract ourselves and no running away from or avoiding the incessant ups and downs of life. The mindfulness meditation tradition is the ultimate "no-frills" method.

Mindfulness meditation is sometimes described as moment-to-moment awareness. In this tradition we are challenged to remember that the present moment is the only moment we can be alive in. The present moment is the only moment we have any kind of dominion over. However, while there is a fundamental simplicity in the practice of mindfulness it is certainly not easy. It requires commitment and perseverance, the willingness to come back again and again to the present moment. The pull to think, ruminate, remember, plan and fantasize is so strong in all of us that being regularly in the present moment is probably the hardest thing we can do. There is a famous and much redrawn cartoon image that expresses this beautifully: a wizened old monk sitting on his meditation cushion says to a rather puzzled-looking young monk, "Nothing happens next, this is it."

In Pali, the language that Shakyamuni Buddha, the historical buddha, spoke the word "buddha" meant an Awakened One: that is, someone who has woken up. All the methods and techniques that the Buddha taught were designed to help his followers to experience this awakening. The Greek philosophers were teaching at the same time the importance of living an "examined" life in order to know oneself. The Buddha taught a practical method for doing this and it did not stop at knowing oneself. The path of awakening begins with the mindfulness practice of cultivating awareness in meditation; this becomes the base for the generation of the necessary wisdom and method for engaging skillfully in the world. There is a marvelous four-line traditional Zen poem that captures the essence of how this path of awakening flows from the willingness to practice moment-to-moment awareness:

To know oneself
Is to forget oneself
And to forget oneself
Is to be Enlightened by all things.[1]

The practice of mindfulness comes directly from the techniques and insights taught by the Buddha, but it is not a religious or even a spiritual practice. It does not require you to take on any beliefs, esoteric worldviews, or rituals. Mindfulness meditation involves having a commitment to being present to how things are, not to how we want them to be; feeling how we feel rather than trying to feel a particular way. A meditator using this practice cultivates a willingness to say, no matter what is happening, "*This* is how it is."

The word "practice" is generally used when referring to what a meditator is doing. It is important to understand what this means: it does not mean rehearsing, it does not mean earnestly working at meditation to somehow get better and better. It is about being wakeful, alert, and present in each moment as much as possible. It is also about remembering to come back to that present moment awareness, to come back again and again and again whenever you notice that you have become lost—in memories, plans, emotions, sensations, projects, thoughts, fantasies, and ruminations.

Mindfulness meditation involves cultivating a patient, open-hearted, non-judging quality, and we are generally not good at doing this. Most of our life we spend being out of the moment because seeing how it really is can often be painful and distressing. This habit of unawareness comes from our clinging and grasping after security, our wanting things to be other than how they are. The reality that the Buddha awakened to was impermanence: no matter how hard we try, things keep changing; absolutely nothing is fixed and certain. Loved ones get sick, we all get old, everyone dies, our savings and superannuation cannot ensure our safety, careers falter, friends betray us, the memory fades. Of course we have our joys and delights too: deep friendships, blissful intimacies, epiphanies in nature. But we clutch at them feverishly, wanting them to go on forever.

At the beginning of this book, I noted that one of the first and often most alarming difficulties we confront when starting to meditate is the seemingly wild, untamed quality of the mind. That first experience is generally the conditioned surface restlessness of the mind. As we continue to meditate we begin to notice at a deeper level how effortlessly the mind gets caught up with thoughts and memories of the past or with plans and projects for the future. We can see how much of our mental activity is absorbed in past and future thinking. We are only fleetingly in the now. Even when we are immersed in activities that require a lot of present-moment awareness—caring for a baby, driving a car, using a computer—we find ways to "space out" and go on automatic. It is as if we constantly get lost in our memories, our plans and our projects. We can see this quality in an exaggerated form in people who are highly imaginative, dreamy or vague. But even practical and alert people who function at a high level also start to notice how little time they spend in the present.

Having read all this you may still be thinking, "Why is it so important to be in the moment?" When you first practice mindfulness you may be shocked to realize how much of your life you have missed. Because of our mental absences, our vagueness, our entrenched habits of avoiding things that make us feel uncomfortable we fail to experience fully so much of our lives. Years can pass in a haze. Our children grow up before we notice; friends move on; suddenly it seems we have a paunch, grey hair and wrinkles. Where did it all go? Because we take so much for granted, because we are so obsessed with creating safety and security, we miss so much. One of the saddest experiences of my professional life was sitting with an old man who was dying, when he turned to me and asked, "What was all that about, Bob?" My experience is that so many people die, as the saying goes, well-known to their friends and a mystery to themselves. This is a terribly painful result of our chronic inability to be alive in the present moment, to be present to the way things are, rather than lost in our chronic habit of yearning for things to be another way.

One compelling benefit of cultivating mindfulness is that if we are ever going to accomplish the things we aspire to, we can only do it by being in the present. If we really want to love someone we can only do it by being fully with and present to the other person. If we want to heal, it can only be done now: healing can never be a project for the future. Think of all the other deep aspirations of life: peace of mind, wisdom, compassion, bliss, wakefulness, ecstatic experiences, to name a few. These can only be cultivated and experienced when we are fully awake and alive to the present moment.

In my clinical practice I regularly witness my clients' lives shifting dramatically when they begin to cultivate the willingness to practice a non-choosing awareness in mindfulness meditation. It never comes easily, but the hard-won ability to stay more regularly present can be deeply transformative. I remember working with a young woman with advanced cancer who really took to the practice of meditation. I still vividly remember her saying to me shortly before her death, at a time when she was experiencing high levels of pain and physical discomfort, "You know, Bob, being in the moment is magic."

Many years later a middle-aged man with advanced secondary cancer recounted to me how he had to take time away from his family to be by himself at the beach. One day, only months before he died, he described with a sense of awe and wonder how he had been sitting on the beach, as he did for many hours a day, when he "heard" the tide turn. He felt that this awareness could only have come from his ability to stay in the present moment. Sadly, he went on to observe how completely uninterested his family was in what was for him a numinous experience. For both of these people the ability to stop fighting the flow of life enabled them to approach death with a calm and peaceful attitude.

LEARNING TO BE PRESENT

How can we train ourselves to be more fully awake and present to a moment-by-moment awareness? In chapter two the three principal methods of meditation are outlined. The first one is concentration. Concentration is a very important skill when we begin to train the mind and it provides a good base for the cultivation of mindfulness. The problem is that concentration can be a very tight and rigid form of meditation when used on its own. Mindfulness practice focuses on training awareness in a lighter, more panoramic form of attention than the constriction of concentration, which tries to focus exclusively on an object. When concentration is used in this way it requires a great deal of training and can be tiring.

Traditionally it is taught that there are four foundations for cultivating the practice of mindfulness: mindfulness of the body, mindfulness of feelings, mindfulness of thoughts and emotions and mindfulness of the mind. In the rest of this chapter I focus on cultivating the practice of mindfulness of the body. Chapter seven focuses on extending the mindfulness practice by incorporating the other three foundations of training.

We begin the training in mindfulness by choosing to focus awareness on a part of our experience. This is a first step only:

remember that the goal is to bring all of our experience within the ambit of our meditative awareness. Nothing is excluded; nothing is considered unmanageable. However, we need to train in doing this patiently and slowly. We have been running from and avoiding much of our experience for a long time. It is wise to go step by step: we begin with cultivating awareness of the body because that is the easiest place to start. Sensations, emotions, feelings and thoughts are increasingly subtle in their experience and it is more skillful to bring them into our mindfulness practice when we have established skill in focusing awareness on the body.

MINDFULNESS OF THE BODY

The first foundation of mindfulness meditation focuses on observing and staying connected to the body. Some methods of meditation promote out-of-the-body experiences; mindfulness meditation focuses on having an in-the-body experience. In its essence, mindfulness meditation is about incorporating all the energies of the mind and body into the meditation. The word "mindfulness" itself implies that the mind is fully present—in this case fully present to the body. The focus on the body is centered on the coming and going of the breath. The breath animates the whole body; we can feel the rise and fall of the breath, especially in the trunk and the nostrils. That movement and touch of the breath is the place where we begin to train awareness to stay in the present moment, breath by breath.

The focus on the breath in mindfulness meditation is quite gentle and panoramic. The phrase "bare attention" is sometimes used to describe this method of focus to distinguish it from the sense of rigid intensity implicit in the use of concentration techniques. Bare attention suggests that awareness is rested on the breath in a light and relaxed way, and when the focus is lost or distracted onto something else, that is noted gently and the attention returned consciously but lightly to the breath. The focus is on feeling the breath in the body. Whenever you become aware that you have lost the focus on the breath you note whatever has taken your attention away, without commentary or elaboration, and simply come back to the breath. There is no drama, no militancy, no feeling of failure; the distracting object is simply noted in its essence and the attention gently returned to the breath. It requires a lot of practice to do this effortlessly. As you persevere with this first step of the mindfulness training you build a firm base for extending your meditation practice to include all the other aspects of experience: sensations, feelings, emotions and thoughts. In this practice of meditation you slowly train and refine your awareness to be present to increasingly subtle experiences of body and mind.

The breath is universally used as a focus for attention in meditation. Because the breath and the body are so closely connected, it was assumed in all the great traditions that focusing on the breath was enough to maintain an in-the-body awareness. However, many of us in the West are so disconnected from our bodies that we can watch the breath while our bodies are rigid with tension. That is why it is so helpful to begin your meditation training with a focus on conscious, systematic physical relaxation, as outlined in chapters four and five. The regular practice of a relaxation technique trains the whole body in the art of relaxation. The body can experience again and again how it feels to be deeply at ease. It is an excellent base for cultivating this first step in the practice of mindfulness meditation. When you know what it feels like to be relaxed, and you know how to do it simply and effectively, then your meditation practice can be moved on to the more challenging work of training awareness through the focus on the breath.

It is important to understand that with mindfulness practice your meditation shifts into a more subtle approach. You are not trying to change anything. Observing the breath, training awareness to be present to the body, is the beginning practice for cultivating a non-choosing awareness. You are not moving systematically through the body (as in relaxation meditation), not trying to breathe in a particular way (as in some yoga practices), and not seeking to change the body (as in healing or transformational practices). The great benefit of focusing on the normal natural breath is that it is so deeply connected to the body. The trunk of the body moves with the coming and going of each breath and subtle ripples of the breath flow out into the whole body. We are using a core aspect of everyday life as the focus for meditation rather than having to maintain the effort required to focus on an object like a mantra, a visualization, an image or a prayer.

I describe below some of the breathing techniques that are commonly taught in different traditions. I suggest that after you have read the outline of each technique you pause for ten to fifteen minutes to practice and experience that technique before moving on to the next one. This will give you an opportunity to make a preliminary assessment of each method and help you decide which technique feels most beneficial to you at the present time. Remember to work with the natural rhythm of your breathing, in the moment. You don't need to breathe in a particular way or modify your breathing, unlike yoga practices where great emphasis is placed on specific methods and techniques of breathing.

In mindfulness meditation you work with the natural unforced rhythm of the breath in the body. This is a life-long rhythm. I have found it helpful to remind myself regularly that this breath is in fact my "life breath." The Sufis use a wonderful phrase to enhance this understanding: in their meditation practice they repeat to themselves "this breath is the one that counts." As you work with the breath in this way you will begin to notice a lot more about it. The breath constantly changes: sometimes it is intense, sometimes labored, sometimes slight and fine; sometimes it is longer on the out-breath and at other times longer on the in-breath, stronger in one nostril for a while then stronger in the other. As you train your awareness it will slowly become more subtle and finely focused to notice these constantly changing elements of your experience.

USING THE BREATH AS A FOCUS

FEELING THE BREATH

Feeling the touch of the breath is probably the most universally used method of focusing on the breath in meditation. The instruction is to observe the sensation of the breath as it comes and goes in the body. Establish your attention at first on a simple awareness of the breath, then focus your awareness more acutely by observing the place in your body where you feel that movement of the breath most strongly.

Anchor your attention to a bodily awareness of the breath as it comes and goes. The location of the felt sensation of the breath can vary from session to session. Some of the most common places that people feel this moving touch of the breath in the body are the nostrils, the top lip below the nostrils, the belly or the chest, the rim of the nostrils, a swirling tumbling movement of the breath in the body, an alternating sensation of warmth and coolness in the nostrils.

Your awareness stays focused on the touch of the breath in that place in your body for the rest of the session. As soon as you notice that you have lost your focus, gently bring your attention back to feeling the breath in that place in your body.

In this method the focus of awareness is the sensation of the breath. Rather than *think about* the breath you focus on simply *feeling* the breath as it comes and goes, breath by breath. If you notice the mind wandering, note whatever it is that your attention has gone to and come back to the breath. Simply note the object and come back to the breath every time you become aware that your awareness has shifted from the breath. There is no self-criticism or harsh, intense concentration involved. Focusing on feeling the breath rather than labeling it helps you to lessen the pull of mentation. Cultivating the practice of simply noting the object of distraction is an antidote to our life-long mental habit of commentary and elaboration.

Stay connected to feeling the whole breath, feeling the full movement of the in-breath and the out-breath. You can then refine your attention to even more subtle levels of awareness by noticing the beginning, the middle and the end of each in-breath and out-breath. Notice as well the small pauses in breathing when the breath turns. In the moving rhythm of your breathing the pause between the breaths is a small moment of stillness where there is no felt sensation of the breath for the briefest moment. Over time you may be able to take your awareness a little deeper by noting, when you return your awareness to the breath, whether it is to an in-breath or an out-breath, and even whether it is to the beginning, middle, or end of a breath.

This practice of feeling the breath with a light panoramic attention, simply noting any object of distraction and returning gently to the feeling of the breath, is called practicing "bare attention." It requires diligent practice to gain some confidence and mastery and is the basis for practicing insight meditation. You might like to take some time to sit quietly for ten or more minutes and practice it now.

LABELING THE BREATH

There are many ways of labeling the breath as a method of focusing and training attention in meditation. A label is linked to the in-breaths and the out-breaths and is silently repeated in the mind in synchronization with the flow of the breathing. In the practice of mindfulness and bare attention it is sometimes said that if you have a really agitated busy-mind day you can label the breath "in" and "out" silently in the mind to focus attention more tightly for a while. The instruction is to focus most of your attention on feeling the breath in your body and only a small amount of your attention on the label.

Other label-pairs that are often taught and used are: breathing in, breathing out; calm (in), relaxed (out); renewing (in), releasing (out); letting (in), go (out); peace (in), love (out). The possibilities are as wide as your imagination.

One problem with using a label for the breath in this way is that you can easily fall into a dull routine, saying the label over and over while the mind is spaced out and lost in unawareness. Another potential problem with labeling the breath is that it keeps the mind in a conceptual, thinking mode. Focusing on feeling the breath provides a more fundamental focus that helps cut the life-long habit of mentation. However, labeling is a technique that is widely taught and used and many people find it very helpful. It can be particularly helpful if you have a very active and busy mind. It can also be helpful at the start of a period of meditation to settle and focus your mind away from its earlier immersion in your daily activities. You can use the labeling technique for a few minutes, then gently let go of the label and focus on the simple movement and touch of the life-breath as it comes and goes in your body.

Go ahead and pause now and meditate for a time using whatever pairing of labels appeals to you.

COUNTING THE BREATH

Using a counting technique to anchor attention on the breath is another widely-used technique. It is a good way of focusing and calming a busy mind. Even if you don't use it regularly, it can be helpful to return to a form of counting the breath when all else fails to calm and settle your mind.

The target of counting can be any number of breaths you choose. Common targets to count to are seven, ten, or twenty-one cycles of breathing. The object of attention is the feeling of the breath as you count it. You can do it in two different ways. The first is by counting one and two for the first cycle of in-breaths and out-breaths, three and four for the next, and so on. That is, you count on both the in-breath and out-breath. The second method is to count only on the out-breath, using a cycle of in and out for each count. This is the method I find most helpful.

The fundamental instruction is to go back immediately to the count of one and start again whenever you notice that you have become distracted. Don't try to remember what number in the count you were up to. The goal is to get to the target with a sense of full awareness of each breath as you count it, then go back to one and start again—but getting to your "goal" is completely unimportant; it's the returning to counting itself that matters. This method sounds easy but you will be surprised at how rarely you achieve the goal with full awareness of each breath. You might like to pause for a while to practice this counting technique.

FOCUSING ON THE TOUCH OF THE BREATH

Many meditation lineages and traditions specify that the attention on the sensation of the breath should be focused on one specific place in the body. They can be quite dogmatic about this, arguing that it is the only method permitted in the particular tradition. Some of the common points of focus are: the rim of the nostrils, the space below the nostrils on the upper lip, the movement of the belly, and the rise and fall of the chest. The specific method is often sanctified by saying that it is the exact technique taught by the founder of the lineage and is the quickest way to enlightenment, so it must never be changed. This can be a very seductive appeal. However, remember that while an established tradition of practice is an excellent starting point you do not have to tie yourself to a doctrine that constricts you in cultivating and exploring your own unique experience in meditation. It is said that the Buddha taught thousands of different methods of meditation because he understood that we have such widely varying capabilities and mind-states.

FOCUSING ON THE OUT-BREATH

In this technique you focus only on the out-breath, leaving the in-breath to come of its own accord without any specific focus of attention. The instruction is to keep your awareness focused on the touch and feel of the out-breath, observing how it becomes longer, finer and thinner over time. The whole focus is on the out-breath; the in-breath is left to flow in its own natural rhythm.

It makes sense to focus on the out-breath in this way as it is the "letting-go" part of each cycle of the breath. You are invited to stay constantly focused on that feeling of releasing and letting go on the exhalation, breath after breath. This technique is taught extensively in some of the Tibetan Buddhist meditation traditions. By allowing the in-breath to flow unnoticed and focusing solely on the out-breath, you can cultivate a more panoramic level of awareness. You might like to take a break from reading to experiment with this method now.

COMBINING AN IMAGE WITH THE FOCUS ON THE BREATH

It can be helpful to utilize an image that expresses the commitment to holding the focus on the breath. The willingness to maintain the focus on the breath is like an anchor to awareness. A very helpful image you can use is that of a small boat tied to a buoy and gently moving up and down on the deep ocean swell beneath it. The boat simply rises and falls, connected to the buoy, just as your awareness is connected to the present moment by attending to the ceaselessly moving rhythm of the breath. As you hold this image you can feel the moving breath in your body as akin to the ocean swell that steadily rises and falls beneath the boat. That ocean swell is only a surface above the calmer depths below, just as your breath is the immediate physical experience on the surface of your life while there is an intimation of calmer, stiller depths within.

Take care using imagery in your meditation practice. An image imposes a concept, a thought, onto the breath. Initially it can be a helpful tool to side-step the otherwise excessively busy nature of the mind, but it can also get in the way. Any image, no matter how simple or archetypal, can be a help to some and a hindrance to others. I recall using the image of a small boat tethered to a buoy while I was leading a group in meditation. It was helpful to some members of the group; however, one person who was undergoing chemotherapy treatment found it disturbing as it accentuated their already heaving sensations and nausea. Of course it may also be an alarming image for someone who can't swim or has a strong dislike of the sea.

One image I have found helpful is that of a falcon or kestrel hovering in the air, apparently still except for an occasional small adjustment of a wing tip or tail feather. The bird of prey is completely focused on the possible quarry below. Our attention on the breath can be like that focus of the bird, always seeking to be conscious of when a small adjustment or refinement of awareness is called for.

I was reminded of the power of this image at the time of writing. I have a small cabin which looks out over the countryside to the sea. In front of my window a black-shouldered kite was hunting. It regularly paused, effortlessly hanging in the air, facing into a stiff westerly for many minutes at a time. (This image will not help if you find yourself highly sensitive to the fate of the small creatures that make up the prey of the kite!)

A very helpful image for healing can be breathing in powerful healing light on the in-breath and breathing out all of your disease, depletion and exhaustion as a dark smoky substance on the out-breath. The in-breath can be white or golden or purple or any other healing color, or set of colors, that appeals to you. This practice is set out in more detail in chapter nine. You may like to experiment using other powerful images from your imagination or the natural world to help cultivate your mindful attention to the breath.

LETTING THE BREATH BREATHE YOU

For most of your life the rhythm of your breathing flows without conscious awareness on your part. If you are skillful and attentive you can train yourself to be at one with this deep, flowing rhythm of the life-breath. Awareness and the flowing rhythm of the breath are as one: you simply rest in it, flowing with it. It's like getting in touch with a deeper, more universal rhythm. The seasons and the weather have their natural rhythms and our life too has its seasons and its rhythms. These rhythms are mirrored in the effortless rhythms of our life-breath. When you start to use the breath as a focus for your meditation you can be quite delighted, even surprised, to realize how effortlessly the breath has been breathing you all along. There is no force, no straining: you simply flow with it, breath by breath. You might like to try it for a while now: just let the breath breathe you, resting in mindful awareness breath by breath.

USING THE BODY TO DEEPEN AN AWARENESS OF THE BREATH

Another technique I have found helpful involves starting with the breath and going down into increasingly subtle levels of body awareness, then coming back to the focus on the breath. It is a process of slow, attentive connecting with deep and profound rhythms of the body.

You start by settling your body and mind and then observing the breath for three or four minutes. The instruction is to observe the rhythm of the breath in the body—all its aspects and sensations. Notice all the places in the body that move with or are touched by the sensation of the breath, the many ways that the breath can be experienced. Immerse yourself in the feel of the breath coming and going in the body. The focus is especially on the rhythmic quality of the breath, the deep, natural life-long rhythm of the body. After doing this for a few minutes, let go of the focus on breathing and take your awareness deeper into your body to find a feeling of the pulse.

You may have to search through your body because the sensation of the pulse can be very subtle. You may even need to touch the pulse somewhere with your fingertips in order to have a physical point of focus. You then rest awareness for another three or four minutes on this feeling of the pulse. In focusing on the pulse in this way you refine your awareness to a more subtle level, resting attention on another vital life-long rhythm of the body: the steady beating of the heart.

After a few minutes let go of the focus on the pulse and go deeper to connect with an even more subtle focus of attention: the vibrational energy of the body. By this I mean an awareness of the life-force, the ceaseless flow of energy, sensation, and vibration in the body that animates us and knits the very fabric of our being together. Rest awareness on the body's vibrational energy for a further three or four minutes. At the end of that time let go of that focus and return your attention to the coming and going of the breath using one of the techniques described previously. This technique, taking about ten minutes, can help to refine and sensitize your bodily awareness and help deepen your ability to stay in the moment.

THE NINE-ROUND BREATHING TECHNIQUE

This is another technique that can help to settle your mind and stabilize your focus on the breath as a precursor to a more sustained period of practicing bare attention and mindfulness. In this practice you imagine that you can alternate your breathing through one nostril at a time. It can also help you to gain more control of and focus on your breathing over time. For three rounds of breathing, imagine as distinctly as you can that you breathe in through the left nostril and out through the right. For the next three rounds of breathing, reverse the process: breathe in through the right nostril and out through the left. In the final three rounds of breathing, focus on breathing in and out through both nostrils. It can be very helpful to use this simple focusing technique for a few minutes at the beginning of a meditation session.

In some yoga practices this alternate breathing practice is done using a finger to block the nostril so as to force the breath to flow in the other nostril. In the nine-round breathing practice you use your mental focus only to imagine as strongly as you can the breath flowing in the designated nostril. This technique can be helpful if your mind is agitated or excessively active. On these days you can do a few rounds of this nine-round technique before proceeding to your main meditation practice. You might like to pause to try it now for a few minutes.

EXERCISE

MINDFULNESS OF THE BODY

Set aside about twenty minutes to practice cultivating mindfulness of the body by focusing on the breath. Remember, the aim is to train awareness to be more in the present moment by cultivating the commitment to come back again and again to the felt sensation of the breath.

As you settle into your posture for meditation, be clear about your motivation. (In a recording, leave a pause to establish your motivation.) Feel your presence in the place where you are, your willingness to be in the here and now, on the spot, in the present moment. Feel the touch and pressure of your body with the chair and the floor. Notice the coming and going of any sounds you may hear. (Leave a longer pause.)

Now take a few moments to relax your body more completely. Drop your shoulders some more, soften in the belly, the hands soft and relaxed, the whole weight of your body effortlessly flowing down through the buttocks, thighs, legs and feet into the gentle steady pull of gravity; easy and relaxed. (Pause for thirty seconds.)

Now bring your attention to your breathing. Become more focused on the touch and rhythm of the breath in your body. Notice where you can feel that touch of the breath most strongly in your body today. Is it in the nostrils? the belly? the chest? Wherever it is you can use that place as the focus of awareness. Become aware of the touch of the breath in that place as it comes and goes in the body. Let that touch and feel of the breath be the focus of your attention, feeling the full movement and sensation of each in-breath and each out-breath. (Pause for one minute.)

Whenever you notice your attention has shifted or got lost, bring it back to the breath, simply and gently. Keep coming back to feeling the touch of each breath in that place in your body. Become more aware of the fullness of each breath: how each in-breath and out-breath has a beginning, a middle and an end. Notice the momentary pause, a moment of stillness, when the breath turns. Do this for ten to fifteen minutes.

Variation: Notice where your attention is now and bring it back to the breath. Notice if you are coming back to an in-breath or an out-breath. Be fully present to each breath. (Pause for a few more minutes.) Notice where your attention is now. Before you finish see if you can give your complete attention to each breath for the last minute. (Pause for one minute.) Bring the meditation to a close now by taking a few deep, full, slow breaths, slowly stretching and moving your body as you breathe out each time.

In doing this exercise you are cultivating the first foundation of mindfulness and practicing bare attention. Bare attention helps you to keep returning to the anchor of the breath without force, strain or duress; it is the practice that makes mindfulness possible. It is the beginning of a deep retraining to relate to what is rather than how you want it to be.

chapter 7

Deepening the Practice of Mindfulness

The practice of mindfulness meditation focuses on our actual life experiences rather than a single object of concentration. Mindfulness takes the experiences of our life and helps us to establish a meditative understanding of, and relationship with, these experiences. As we build confidence in this practice two things start to stand out. Firstly, we become more skilled at noticing what is present in our life. In mindfulness meditation, the instruction is to keep coming back to the present moment, observing what is here rather than what we would like to be here. Secondly, we notice what happens to all the experiences of our life as we observe them. We begin to see that things don't last very long. The breath never stays the same; sensations in the body come and go, and increase and decrease in intensity; emotions are fluid and constantly changing; the mind is forever moving between the past and the future with only the briefest stops in the present.

In the practice of mindfulness meditation we cultivate a willingness to be open and present to all the parts of our life experience. In the previous chapter we looked at the first foundation of the practice of mindfulness meditation: mindfulness of the body. We have to learn how to be at home in our body as that will support us in being at home in the present moment. Focusing on the physical sensation of the breath gives us a method to stay in the present moment. The practice of coming back again and again to the touch and the feel of the breath, being centered on the breath, enables us to stay in the reality of the present moment. In this way our meditation begins to be very practical, a way of being rather than a formal repetitive exercise.

When we attain a degree of stability in our focus on the breath, we can then move on to deepen the practice of mindfulness by working successively with mindfulness of feelings and sensations, mindfulness of moods and emotions, and finally mindfulness of the mind. With each step we broaden the meditation focus toward the goal of being able to maintain a stillness in the midst of all our life experiences. Nothing is excluded; nothing is considered to be unmanageable. We do not have to create ideal conditions in order to meditate. We no longer use our meditation as a kind of subtle aggression against ourselves in the never-ending pursuit of change and self-improvement.

MINDFULNESS OF SENSATIONS AND FEELINGS

In this further development of mindfulness the goal is to work with all the diverse energies and sensations in the body. Most of us are deeply conditioned not to feel or be open to our bodies, particularly to things that are distressing or painful. In my practice as a psychologist I frequently meet people who are even afraid of things that may give delight and pleasure. In many ways we have learned to distance ourselves from our bodies and to avoid noticing what the body is feeling.

One of the Buddha's fundamental insights was the pervasiveness of pain and suffering in the world. This is the first noble truth of the Buddha's very first teaching that has come to be known as the Four Noble Truths. The Buddha also taught about the causes of suffering, the pathway out of suffering and the power of love and compassion. While the Buddha challenges us to look clearly at our own experiences and the world around us to see the universal experience of suffering, he was also relentlessly optimistic in describing how we can realize our human potential to awaken. The meditation that he taught had as its essence a method to stop and look clearly at our minds, our experiences and the world around us.

A common saying in China is the observation that life is made up of the ten-thousand joys and the ten-thousand sorrows. That seems to be the deal we get in this life: pleasure and joys mixed up with pain and sorrows. If we are lucky we get a reasonable balance of both. However, we spend a lot of our energy trying to avoid and run away from the pain and sorrows.

Logically, it's crazy being so fearful about things we all have to experience if we are going to be alive on this planet. The truth is we can never avoid suffering and we can never succeed in making the world go our way. Our attempts to contain and control the sorrows and pains of life can lead to a constricted, withdrawn and narrowed experience of life, and even then pain and sorrows have an infinite range of possibilities to breach our defenses. The same applies for the joys and pleasures of life: some days we simply find ourselves being happy for no good reason at all.

In the practice of mindfulness we train ourselves to sit in meditation and take what we get. We no longer meditate as a type of improvement plan. The practice is predicated on a willingness to accept that *I am who I am*, and to meditate patiently to enter into a better relationship with all our parts. The practice is simply to be open in a curious and attentive way to any sensation or feeling in the body that may become strong or noticeable.

If there is pain, we notice it. Likewise, if there is itching, burning, throbbing, aching, flatulence, heat or cold, or any other strong sensation, we train ourselves to observe the sensation with an attentive patience and interest. The best way to do this is to label the sensation as simply as you can and observe its presence in your body. When you start to do this in meditation you will learn a lot about your habitual patterns and the nature of difficult physical sensations. A particular sensation may intensify as you observe it; it may change or lessen or even go away. Your task is to stay open to whatever happens, practising a non-choosing awareness, simply open to what is. It takes a lot of patient practice and perseverance to deepen the mindfulness practice in this way.

Remember, in mindfulness meditation the anchor is the breath. Always return to the flowing sensation of the breath to continuously stabilize awareness. The essence of the instructions for this step in cultivating mindfulness is to notice whenever there is a sensation in the body that is stronger than the breath. You then let go of the focus on the breath and focus your attention on the sensation and its location in the body, labeling it simply, for example, as *throbbing, throbbing, throbbing,* or *burning, burning,* or *itching, itching, itching.* You label it with the simplest and most appropriate word you can think of. You stay with the simple patient labeling of the sensation while it is present in your body and stronger than the breath. When the sensation fades you take your attention back to the breath.

When we start to do this it can seem counter-intuitive, even foolhardy, to focus our attention deliberately by meditating on something we have been avoiding or fearing for most of our life. At first the pain or discomfort we have been avoiding may intensify when we focus on it, which can be alarming. Sometimes the pain or discomfort will lessen in intensity, but can still be quite unpleasant. It may also change location in the body, lessen and slowly fade. Whatever happens, remember the basic instruction: while the sensation is stronger than the breath endeavor to observe its presence and location in your body and continue to label it simply. You may need to change the label to mirror the changing experience of the sensation in the body; for example, a throbbing sensation might become a twisting sensation and then become an itch before it lessens and fades.

Don't make this practice a torture for yourself. You are endeavoring to do something challenging and difficult. It takes time and some courage to become confident with this practice. Pain and discomforting physical sensations can have a solid and persistent quality. It is a good idea to practice with little aches, pains and irritations in the body before you tackle the really big pains. If you do a lot of meditation regularly you will always have aches and pains in the knees, buttocks, back and ankles to work with. And of course there are the regular itches, daily discomforts and muscular twitching to work with as well.

There is a further instruction that will help to make this aspect of the mindfulness practice a little more manageable. If you get lost in the pain or discomfort, if it feels too strong and unmanageable or even overwhelming, then let go of the focus on the physical sensation and take your attention back to the breath. This is the fundamental instruction for all levels of the mindfulness practice: whenever you get lost, lose your focus, feel frightened or overwhelmed, go back to the breath.

By doing this you stabilize yourself and center your attention to the present moment. It may take quite a lot of practice before you can approach the big pains. Remember that the goal is to gain an experiential understanding that all the problems of your life are manageable and workable. You will notice how even the most difficult things can change when you turn toward them and observe their moment to moment qualities, experiencing them as impermanent, ceaselessly changing phenomena rather than fixed, solid and almost concrete experiences in the body.

E X E R C I S E

MINDFULNESS OF THE SENSATIONS AND FEELINGS IN THE BODY

Before you begin, go through the settling, relaxing and focusing activities set out in the mindfulness meditation exercise on page (82).

When you are relaxed, with good posture, just rest in that state for a while, easy and relaxed. Be here and on the spot, experiencing your own presence, where you are right now. If you can hear any sounds that threaten to be intrusive see if you can simply note them—hearing, hearing, hearing—while they are persistent. Otherwise, just notice the background polyphony of sounds coming and going. (In a recording, pause for thirty seconds.)

Gently bring your attention to the breath. It may feel like returning to an old familiar object of awareness. Notice the flow and touch of the breath in your body. Become aware of where you have the strongest sensation of the breath's touch in your body. Center your awareness on the sensation of the breath at that place in your body, feeling the fullness of each in-breath and each out-breath, staying with the movement and touch of each breath in your body. (Pause for one minute.)

If you become aware of any feeling or sensation in your body that is stronger than the breath, let go of the focus on your breathing and focus your awareness on that sensation in your body, observing clearly its location in your body and labeling it as simply as you can: itching, itching, itching; or throbbing, throbbing; or burning, burning, burning—whatever label is appropriate. Stay with it, labeling it simply while it is stronger than the breath. When it passes or softens bring your attention back to the breath. (Pause for a few minutes.)

Whenever there is a feeling or sensation in your body that is stronger than the breath, bring your attention to that feeling or sensation, observing it and labeling it simply while it is present. Don't get caught in any commentary or story about the sensation; simply observe it and label it while it is there and stronger than the breath. Keep coming back to the breath. Your awareness of the flowing movement and touch of each breath is your anchor. (Pause for five or six minutes.)

Now notice where your attention is at this moment. Bring it back to the breath and see if you can stay fully present to each breath for the last couple of minutes. (Pause for two minutes.)

Before you finish, take some time to change the rhythm of your breathing by taking some slow, fuller, deeper breaths, moving and flexing your limbs as you exhale. Open your eyes gently when you are ready.

MINDFULNESS OF MOODS AND EMOTIONS

To be human is to know the intensity of the moods, feelings, and emotions that can sweep over us, often unexpectedly. These moods and emotions flavor and color our whole world. When you are sad the world seems tainted with sadness; when you are light-hearted and joyous you can put a positive spin on almost any experience. In chapter three, I outlined the five common hindrances we can experience to our meditation practice: desire, aversion, sloth and torpor, restlessness, and doubt. These hindrances are all associated with strong moods and emotions; however, desire and aversion are the categories that contain most of the powerful emotions that threaten our burgeoning equanimity.

Desire involves all the things we want and crave, the fantasies we have about how happy we will be when we get them. Our consumerist society is caught up in the allure of increasingly clever advertising, with its seductive suggestion that if you get this thing it will help you to be happy. We rarely listen to our experience: what we get doesn't make us happy, it just seems to lead to another cycle of desire.

Aversion is the experience of all the powerful negative emotions that can so strongly grip us. We have all met people who have allowed their life to be dominated by feelings of resentment, ill will, anger, boredom, rage or a corrosive cynicism. These strong negative emotions have the power to ruin friendships, families, workplaces and even whole communities. If we leave them unaddressed in ourselves they can destroy any semblance of calm and equanimity.

In this further extension of the mindfulness practice we aim to observe these strong emotions rather than get caught up in and absorbed by them. As we do this we begin to notice their impermanent nature, how they arise and pass away, often to be replaced by another strong emotion, and then another. Physical sensations in the body can initially feel very fixed and solid, but moods and emotions have a much more evanescent, changing quality about them. Emotions do not last as long as physical feelings and sensations and when we observe them with a mindful awareness they tend to slip away into a cascading flow of other similar, linked emotions.

The problem is that strong emotions also have a "sticky" quality about them: they have a habit of coming back again and again. Difficult emotions often have a persistent churning quality about them. It can take months, even years of practice to successfully soften the grip of a powerful emotion in our life.

When we have gained some skill incorporating sensations in the body into our meditation practice we can move into working more consciously with emotions and moods. The practice is to embrace these moods and emotions, look at them, feel where they sit in the body and gently label them as long as they are present. Again, the practice is to name them as simply as you can, free of any commentary, free of the story about them, the life-long melodrama about them.

To strengthen our commitment to the path of awakening we need to be able to sit with these different emotional states as they arise in our meditation and be willing to feel them: to feel anger, hatred, boredom, apathy, dread, fear, sadness, joy, delight, rapture, grief, lust and many more emotions, whenever they are present. We note where we feel these emotions in the body, and we label each emotion to observe the changing feelings associated with that emotion in the body. This practice offers us the deepest possibility of opening our heart. Over time, with diligent practice, we are more able to see that these emotions are not obstacles to the path—they are the path. Opening again and again to these emotions and moods that come up from deep within us eventually enables us to open out to the whole world.

We tend to have a view of ourselves and others that solidifies and fixes these emotions. People are often described by others or themselves as being an angry person, a sad person, or a fearful person. This can lead to passivity and feelings of defeat about the power of these strong emotions in our life. We forget that these apparently fixed emotional states are the result of the circumstances of our life. They resulted from adaptations we have made over the course of our life and they can be changed, albeit with considerable diligence and effort. The essence of this aspect of the mindfulness meditation practice is a growing ability to feel and observe the emotion without being caught in it. It's like saying, "I *have* this emotion but I *am not* this emotion."

I once had a client who described how he had hated his mother all his life. His father had died years before and he deeply grieved his life-long inability to be close to him. But he felt his mother was stupid and docile. All his life he had been filled with venomous rage toward her. Now, my client was in his early forties and his mother had a rapidly progressing dementia. He even fantasized that she would be knocked down and killed on her nightly wanderings. When my client visited his mother the first time after finding her a place in a nursing home, he was shocked to come upon her dribbling, highly confused and unable to recognize him.

It was this observation of the rawest suffering that melted my client's heart. In that moment he was able to let go of a lifetime of resentment and rage and simply embrace his mother with the pure love and affection that had been absent all his life. Our intense, reverberating emotions are like that man's. However, we do not have to wait for a sudden, unexpected event in our life to shift them. We can use our willingness to extend our meditation practice and incorporate this third foundation of mindfulness meditation to loosen and lighten the grip of distress and disturbing emotions on our life.

The practice follows the steps already described. If, while sitting in meditation working with the breath to stay in the present moment, a strong emotion or movement of the heart comes up, the instruction is to let go of the focus on the breath, observe the emotion and simply name it while it is present. Name what is present quietly and softly in the mind; at the same time be willing to feel with gentleness and curiosity where it may be present in the body. This extension of the practice of mindfulness in our meditation can be an expression of our commitment to training and refining awareness, to be present to all the experiences of our life.

As you build your confidence in this practice, you will notice that emotions can quickly change. One emotion might shift into another and then into another before the intensity softens and fades and you can return to the breath. For example, anger might change to resentment, which might change to sadness, then to grief and finally to loneliness. Your meditation practice is to keep tracking and naming these emotions while they stay strongly present. If the emotions get too strong and you feel you may be caught up in them or lost in them, return your attention to the breath and stay mindfully present to the touch of each breath while the strong emotion sits powerfully in the background. It may take months, even years, for you to make a dent in your lifetime identification with certain strong and persistent emotions; but be assured it *can* be done!

EXERCISE

MINDFULNESS OF EMOTIONS AND MOODS

Set aside twenty to twenty-five minutes to extend the practice of your mindfulness meditation: Your primary focus stays centered on the breath but is open to noting and observing any strong sounds, feelings, emotions or moods that may arise.

Take a few minutes to settle yourself into your chosen posture, strong and present and alert. Clarify your motivation and slowly soften and relax your body. (In a recording, pause for two to three minutes.)

Now be aware of where you can most noticeably feel the touch and movement of the life breath again. Gently settle your attention on the fullness of each in-breath and each out-breath. (Pause for one minute.)

If you notice any sensations or feelings in your body that are stronger than the breath, let go of the focus on the breath and notice them fully, labeling them simply as aching or cold or throbbing or itching or any label that describes what is present. When they pass, turn your attention back to the next breath, but stay with the sensations as long as they are present and stronger than the breath. If any strong sounds arise, don't get caught in commentary, simply note that you are hearing, hearing, hearing as long as it lasts. When the sound or sensation passes always bring your attention back to the breath, back to the fullness of each in-breath and out-breath. (Pause for one or two minutes.)

If any strong emotions or moods come—like anger, fear, loneliness, desire, lust, boredom and so on—let go of the focus on the breath and name the emotions softly in the mind while you feel them as fully as you can: *wanting, wanting, wanting, or fear, fear, fear.* As long as the emotion or mood is present, name it. Note how one emotion or mood flows into another and simply keep observing it and labeling it. Then when the emotion fades, turn your attention back to the next breath. Continue to do this for the next ten minutes or so. (Pause for one or two minutes.)

Remember to stay in the present. Don't let the mind wander off. Always come back to the breath, to sensations in the body, to any strong emotions or moods. (Pause for four or five minutes.)

Remember to keep the naming soft and spacious. Keep most of your attention on feeling the touch of the breath, the sensation in the body, the feeling of the mood or emotion. Keep noticing whatever is present. (Pause for one or two minutes.)

Before you end, take a few moments to notice where your attention is. In the last minute or two focus on either the fullness of each breath or the seamless flow of emotions and moods as they come and go, one following another. (Pause for one or two minutes.)

To finish the meditation take some deeper, fuller breaths, right down into the bottom of your lungs, and as you breathe out, slowly stretch and move your limbs and trunk. End the meditation with a refreshed alertness, taking a moment to pause and dedicate your efforts before you finish.

MINDFULNESS OF THE MIND

The ceaseless flow of thoughts in our mind seems to have a life and an energy of its own. When we stop to notice we can observe how we ceaselessly judge, remember, regret, plan, ruminate and think. Behind the constant flow of thoughts are our attitudes and beliefs. These sit deeply in our mind and flavor all our thoughts, yet they are largely unexamined by us. We generally only become aware of how strong and entrenched an attitude or belief is in our mind when someone challenges us or points it out. In this final foundation of mindfulness meditation we begin to train ourselves to notice the quality and activity of the mind with an attentive and receptive interest. I have heard it called "inward listening," which beautifully captures the essence of this final step in the mindfulness practice.

We start by patiently training ourselves in meditation to be aware of and awake to the movements of our mind without seeking to censor or change it. We simply notice what the mind is doing and name it whenever we find that we have lost the focus on the breath. This is the reverse of what we normally do. Normally our thoughts have a life of their own, coming and going at will, while we remain imprisoned in attitudes and opinions that are largely unknown to us.

Over time, as we change our relationship with our thoughts, we can begin to directly experience the truth of the statement that asserts: "While I have thoughts I am not my thoughts." Even more radically, we can begin to observe: "This is not me, it's just *thinking*."

I still remember a client of mine years ago who grew up in a censorious, perfectionist family. As the therapy progressed he became more shocked by the terrible judging quality he now saw behind most of his opinions and behaviors. He had reluctantly agreed to try simply naming and observing this judging mind whenever he noticed it was present. One day he burst into my office exclaiming, "You're right, it's just *thinking* and I can even stop it for a few minutes at a time." This was the deepest "ah ha!" experience of his life up to that time.

When we embark upon this final extension of the mindfulness meditation it is like becoming a witness to our mind, cultivating a patient willingness to observe the activities of the mind. Our usual response to the mind's activities is a complete identification with our thoughts and the accompanying emotion. We effortlessly fall into old, old habits of reactiveness, fear, resentment, wanting, planning and judging. It takes great patience and kindness to step back from this deeply habitual pattern into a more detached witnessing position.

It is no accident that observing the workings of our mind is the final step in cultivating insight through the practice of mindfulness. The workings of our mind are highly complex, subtle and often unknown to us. This is even more so if we have never engaged in self-reflection. As we patiently enter into this aspect of the practice of mindfulness meditation we can start to learn more about how our mind works, seeing the patterns of our thoughts, responses and reactions. As our meditation deepens and we become more confident we can also notice a quality of stillness and silence that sometimes arises. This can be a beautiful, even blissful, experience; yet when we observe it we notice that it too passes.

In the East meditation teachers frequently use powerful metaphors to describe the willful undisciplined quality of the mind. They talk of the "wild elephant mind" and the "monkey mind." It is sometimes said that the mind has many of the qualities of a very naughty, tantrum-throwing three-year-old child. These metaphors and images suggest that there is a primitive wildness about the mind; that no matter how hard we try and how successful we are there will always be a residue of that wild, unpredictable aspect to the mind.

Knowing this we can be more respectful and caring of our mind. We can guard and protect our mind through the practice of ethical and moral behavior, as well as the patient effort to know it and befriend it in the practice of meditation. Understanding and then training the mind through this practice is a long journey. It is really about getting to know yourself in a deep and attentive way, learning to experience your true nature. If you diligently practice in this way, there is every possibility that over time you will become more clear-minded, kind and resolute.

I want to reinforce this last point. It is not easy to work with the mind in this way. Sometimes in your meditation practice you will experience the mind's activities of thinking, judging, planning, or remembering as being extraordinarily insistent, even overwhelming. If it becomes too difficult, let go of the focus on the mind and return to the breath. In the cultivation of mindfulness the breath is the constant anchor for awareness. You should always be ready to return your focus to the breath, to compose and settle yourself with awareness of the breath in a kind, gentle and attentive way.

When you practice mindfulness of the mind in meditation you cultivate a willingness to notice whatever pattern of thinking is strongest at any given moment. Simply label the quality of mind that is present: *thinking, remembering, judging, churning, planning, regretting*. Because your thoughts are endlessly streaming through your mind, the pattern of thinking will normally pass as you label it.

Of course it may return again and again throughout your meditation session. If the thinking pattern is strong, if there is insistent churning, anxiety or worry in the mind, then continue to simply label it while it is present and when it recurs. If you can, try to stay with the simple observing and labeling until it resolves or until your meditation time is over. The Buddha taught that our minds have been out of control, driven by karma and delusion, for millennia. It may take some patient, diligent meditation practice to begin to change that deeply entrenched pattern.

E X E R C I S E

MINDFULNESS OF THE MIND

Put aside about twenty-five minutes for the following practice of mindfulness meditation, which includes the four foundations of mindfulness: the body, the feelings, the emotions and the mind.

Take time to establish a stable and comfortable posture. Be clear about your motivation. Be aware that you have set this time aside to cultivate a mindful awareness of all aspects of your life. Take time to relax and soften your body, paying particular attention to your belly and shoulders. (In a recording, pause for thirty seconds.)

Allow the buttocks and thighs to settle down more fully into their support. Allow yourself to soften in the hands. The head is effortlessly balanced, the jaw relaxed and all the muscles and skin through the face and scalp are soft and long and relaxed, easy and relaxed. (Pause for one minute.)

Now bring your attention to your breathing and once again feel the touch and movement of your life breath. Notice where you can feel the breath most prominently today. Feel the full movement and rhythm of each breath, the beginning, middle and end of each breath. You may even notice how the breath breathes you. Quite effortlessly now, let the breath breathe you and simply notice its touch, breath after breath. (Pause for two minutes.)

The breath is the center and anchor of your meditation. Whenever you notice that your attention has wandered, bring it back to the breath.

If any sounds, feelings, sensations in the body, moods or emotions come up and they are stronger than the breath, let go the focus on the breath and label them simply while they are present: *hearing, hearing; throbbing, throbbing; itching, itching; fear, fear; sadness, sadness.* Label each emotion simply and observe its presence in your body and mind. When it passes come back to the breath. Notice if you are coming back to an in-breath or an out-breath. Don't force the breath in any way. Always allow the breath to settle into its own rhythm. Let the breath breathe you, simply observing its touch and movement in your body. Remember that whatever is happening the breath is always present and flowing. Whenever you get lost, as soon as you notice come back to the breath.

If thinking is present, when you notice the pattern or energy of your thought name it simply: thinking, thinking, thinking; remembering, remembering, remembering; planning, planning, planning. Name it while it is present and strong. Keep the naming simple and when it passes return your attention to the breath. (Pause for one or two minutes.)

When thinking is present name it simply. Sometimes it will fade as soon as you name it; then go back to the next breath. If the thinking or sensation or emotion is strong and insistent stay with it, observing where it is located in your body and labeling it simply while it is present. When it softens and passes, as it will, go back to the breath. (Pause for five or six minutes.)

Note whatever is present, making no effort to change it. Whenever sounds, sensations, moods or thoughts become strong, let go of the breath and label these things as simply as you can, observing them while they are present. When they pass, return to the breath. The breath is the center of your practice; stay with your breath most of the time. Whenever something draws you away from the breath, when your mind wanders into thoughts, observe whatever is there and when it fades return to the next breath. (Pause for five minutes.) Now for the last couple of minutes just notice whatever is present, labeling it simply, focusing on whatever is strongest and feeling its presence. As you do that, notice what happens to it, being present to whatever is here. (Pause for two minutes.)

Now, before bringing the meditation to an end, notice the state of your mind, feelings and emotions. You might like to dedicate whatever qualities of awareness, peacefulness or understanding you have generated for the benefit of yourself and all beings, then take some slow, deep breaths and gently open your eyes.

chapter 8
Meditations for Cultivating a Good Heart

Love and compassion are universally praised. All the major religious and spiritual traditions and the humanist philosophers emphasize their importance. They are the foundation not only for a good quality of life for the individual but also for a humane and civil society both nationally and internationally. This chapter outlines some practical ways you can consciously and systematically cultivate love and compassion in your meditation practice.

In the great meditation traditions of Buddhism, love is defined as the wish for others to be happy and free from the causes of unhappiness. In its essence, love is cultivating a willingness to bring others in close and accord them the status of a friend. We effortlessly wish happiness for our friends and loved ones, and the meditations described in this chapter present methods for slowly extending this wish out to include all beings. Compassion is defined as the wish that others be free of suffering and the causes of suffering. Compassion can only be truly cultivated if we are willing to put ourselves into the place of another; to walk for a mile in their shoes, as the saying goes. Compassion requires empathy: a willingness to stretch our imagination to try and feel what it must be like for another.

In the Christian gospels, Christ's great teaching parables have at their core the primacy of unconditional love and compassion. The parables of the Prodigal Son and the Good Samaritan and the Beatitudes are sublime expressions of the benefits of loving and compassionate action. Shortly before he died, Christ said to his followers that above all else he wanted them to love one another. In our modern times how can we ignore his challenge: "What you do to the least among you, you do it to me."[1]

There is a wonderful story told about the Buddha when he first introduced a meditation on loving-kindness to his followers. During the meditation the Buddha's main attendant and disciple, Ananda, experienced enormous joy and bliss. After the meditation he is reported to have said to the Buddha that now he understood that the practice of loving-kindness was at least half of the path. The Buddha replied, "No, Ananda, it is the whole of the path." The Dalai Lama always seeks to remind us that what distinguishes human beings from all other species is our capacity to help others. He strongly asserts that the greatest use we can make of our life is to dedicate it to helping others.

The practice of love and compassion is most praised and valued when it is universal—offered freely to all beings without exception. Pause for a moment to think through for yourself the implications of cultivating such an attitude. Be clear that universal love and compassion does not mean that wrongdoers should not be punished if they break the law. It does mean, however, that victim and perpetrator are equally deserving of love and compassion. It is a radical idea that challenges our deeply ingrained habit of partiality yet has an inspiring appeal to the highest aspiration we can imagine.

In the Gospels, Christ set the benchmark for the practice of loving-kindness. He said that to practice turning the other cheek seven times in the presence of ill will or persecution was nowhere near enough, it should be done *seventy times seven* times. In the Buddhist tradition, the story about the Buddha's taming of the mass-murderer Angulimala is an example of how the skillful application of love and compassion can tame even the wildest of beings. In the Metta Sutra, the Buddha compiled a long list of blessings that will come to a person who cultivates love and compassion.[2]

The problem is not so much the value of love and compassion, but how we can be more loving and compassionate in our daily lives. The primacy of love and compassion is almost universally accepted. However, they can easily be distorted by a mushy sentimentality, or by bland unthinking repetition, or by a "Yes, but..." rationalisation of why not *everyone* can be treated equally or why some are more deserving of my loving-kindness than others. In the East this rationalizing tendency comes in a more pernicious form: "What can I do? It's their karma to experience that."

Therefore what we need are techniques for cultivating attitudes of love and compassion that counteract our effortless and generally unconscious tendency to rationalize our behavior on the basis of a narrow and self-serving outlook. We need methods to help familiarize our mind with the spontaneous thoughts of love and compassion. If we don't have robust techniques that continually build and reinforce a willingness to practice love and compassion no matter what, we will unconsciously fall back into asking ourselves some version of "What's in it for me?" We all experience the world through the filters of our culture, race, age, gender, status, attitudes, and habits. We need to find a method of cultivating an antidote to partiality, which is a result of experiencing the world through such filters. If we don't we inevitably will cultivate love and compassion only when it suits us, when it is convenient or when it fits with our limited outlook.

The Buddha's path of awakening is founded on the cultivation of both wisdom and "method" through the practices of study, meditation, contemplation, analysis and engagement in the world. Wisdom is the training to overcome our fundamental ignorance, to see things as they really are.[3] *Method* is the cultivation and practice of love and compassion.

It is important to keep our practice of method and wisdom in balance. If we give too much emphasis to the wisdom arm of practice, we can become cold, intellectual and distant. If we give too much emphasis to method, we can be overwhelmed by the suffering and sorrows of the world or lost in sentimentality. Outlined here are some techniques to help you develop a more loving and compassionate outlook, which should have an impact on your life and the lives of all the people you meet.

Mindfulness meditation practice is an excellent and reliable base for making your mind stable and calm. When you have gained a rudimentary capacity to keep your awareness on the breath you can then begin to practice meditations for the cultivation of love and compassion. If you do not have this stability in your meditation practice, it is possible that you will be swept away by the strong feelings and emotions that arise when you begin the conscious and deliberate cultivation of love and compassion in your meditation sessions. Meditation practice is about training the mind and forging a deep transformation within the mind, which takes commitment, time and patience. Remember, when emotions become too strong, when your mind is wild or filled with disturbing thoughts, when you are feeling overwhelmed, let go of whatever practice you are doing and go back to the breath, to the simple focus on the feel of each breath as it comes and goes in the body. When you have stabilized your mind, your feelings and emotions, return your attention to the image or contemplation that you are working with in your meditation.

It is also important to cultivate a moral and ethical view that will support your meditation practice. The Buddha, Jesus Christ, the authors of the Upanishads, Lao Tzu and Confucius all taught that their path of practice was predicated on the commitment to moral and ethical conduct. Your practice of meditation and loving-kindness must be supported by right action and right behavior. The Buddha encouraged all his disciples to live by what are called the five precepts: not killing, not lying, not stealing, not committing sexual misconduct, and not using intoxicants.

For many, a commitment to non-harming is the beginning of the Buddhist path of meditation. The precepts are based on a respect for all life, the rights of others and the core behaviors necessary for a just and civil society. They are also central to calming and training the mind. No matter what your moral and ethical stance is, it is important to have a set of values based on a deep respect for all beings. Then you can cultivate love and compassion as a significant part of your meditation practice. The Buddhist tradition further encourages us to extend our practice of love and compassion over time into the practice of what is called "Great Love" and "Great Compassion": making our aspiration universal, to cover all beings; and making a personal commitment of responsibility to attaining this goal.

PRACTICES FOR THE CULTIVATION OF LOVE AND COMPASSION

THE FOUR IMMEASURABLE WISHES

In this practice, equanimity and sympathetic joy are added to love and compassion to constitute the *four immeasurable wishes*. They are called "immeasurable" because it is impossible to know the full reach and power of their effect in the world. Sympathetic joy is the willingness to want the very best for others and to delight in their good fortune. Surely this is one of the most difficult of things to do: we are all familiar with the plaintive inner voice that pleads, "What about me?"

Equanimity is the willingness to open our heart to everybody without distinction or limitation. It is a practice that starts to break down our deeply entrenched habit of discrimination: we either like, dislike, or are indifferent to all the people we meet. This habit flows from an unexamined, egocentric attitude based on a judgment about how these people appear to us or, more fundamentally, what they do for us.

A very powerful way of slowly familiarizing the mind with this new attitude is to take time to affirm the four immeasurable wishes at the start of your meditation practice.

Each wish has four levels of aspiration. Begin with the first level: "How wonderful it would be." This is like connecting with the wish: "I really like the idea; it would be terrific; it appeals to me." The second level is more committed and strong: "May it happen." At this second level, you really want it to happen; it is no longer simply just a good idea. The third level involves making a personal commitment and accepting responsibility for bringing it about: "I myself will cause it to happen!" At the fourth level you recognize what a huge task you have just committed yourself to and request help from the highest sources of inspiration you can imagine. Some possibilities are: "Please Lord Jesus Christ (or Mother Mary, or buddhas and bodhisattvas, or holy beings, or God, or universal wisdom), help me to be able to do this."

E X E R C I S E

THE FOUR IMMEASURABLE WISHES

This practice involves slowly reciting each aspiration, either silently in your mind or out loud if you wish. Pause for a few moments to reflect on each level of aspiration before moving on to the next one.

THE WISH OF IMMEASURABLE EQUANIMITY

How wonderful it would be if all beings could dwell in equanimity, free from anger and attachment, free from holding some close and others distant.

May all beings dwell in equanimity, free from anger and attachment, free from holding some close and others distant.

I myself will cause all beings to dwell in equanimity, even-minded and open-hearted, realizing their essential equality with all.

Holy beings (or whatever source of inspiration you choose), please help me to be able to do this.

THE WISH OF IMMEASURABLE LOVE

How wonderful it would be if all beings could have happiness and be free from the causes of unhappiness.

May all beings have happiness and be free from unhappiness and its causes.

I myself will cause all beings to have happiness and be free from unhappiness.

Holy beings (or whatever source of inspiration you choose), please help me to be able to do this.

THE WISH OF IMMEASURABLE COMPASSION

How wonderful it would be if all beings were free from suffering and the causes of suffering.

May all beings be free from suffering and its causes.

I myself will cause all beings to be free from suffering and its causes.

Holy beings (or whatever source of inspiration you choose), please help me to be able to do this.

THE WISH OF SYMPATHETIC JOY

How wonderful it would be if all beings were to know the joy of understanding and realizing their full potential.

May all beings know the joy of understanding and realizing their full potential.

I myself will cause all beings to know the joy of understanding and realizing their full potential.

Holy beings (or whatever source of inspiration you choose), please help me to be able to do this.

You might like to add this simple practice at the beginning of your meditation sessions. Remember, the reason for doing a meditation practice like this is to familiarize the mind over and over again with these wishes as an antidote to our usual and deeply conditioned mind of discrimination and self-cherishing. If we don't have a practice like this we tend to be always in thrall to the thought, "What's in it for me?"

In doing this practice it is helpful to be aware of what are described as the four "near enemies" of these immeasurable wishes. The near enemy of love is attachment: feeling that I have to have *this person* or *this thing* for my happiness. The near enemy of compassion is pity: looking down from a superior position and thinking, "Oh, you poor person, let me help you out." The near enemy of sympathetic joy is the comparing mind: "It's not fair, they got a bigger present than me." The near enemy of equanimity is indifference: "Oh that's just their bad luck, these things happen."

Be aware of how these four immeasurable wishes can be easily distorted into their near enemy. When you mistakenly fall into doing the near-enemy practice, don't be surprised if people disparage your efforts and turn away in anger or disgust.

CULTIVATING EQUANIMITY

Equanimity is the foundation attitude for cultivating all good qualities in the mind, and it is vital to developing a more universal practice of love and compassion. The opposite of equanimity is the habit of mind that generates one of these three attitudes: *like, don't like, don't care*. This habit leads us to put other beings into one of three categories: friend, enemy or stranger. As soon as our mind makes one of these distinctions we tend to act accordingly: running after what we like, avoiding what we don't like, and ignoring the rest.

We need to practice regularly and diligently to even begin to break down this deeply entrenched pattern in the mind. Below are four simple practices for the cultivation of equanimity. All four are challenging and you should practice them gently and with a wise choice of situations. Start with small-scale problems that do not generate too much emotion in your mind and heart. Try *not* to fall into a partiality that favors the weak over the strong, the sweet and mild over the rough diamond, the victim over the predator. Do the meditation gently. Don't move your meditation practice too quickly into tough and challenging problems. Exercise the patience and wisdom that knows where your limits are and enables you to extend them a little further month by month, year by year.

CULTIVATING GRATITUDE

You can commit yourself to consciously cultivating an attitude of gratitude on a daily basis. Each day, look for the good in others and seek out things to rejoice in. There is a lovely idea I came across recently, attributed to the German mystic Meister Eckhart. He suggested that if there was only one prayer you said in your entire life and it was "Thank you," then that would be enough.[4]

REFLECTING ON INTERDEPENDENCE

You can include in your regular meditation sessions an analytical or reflective meditation on your interdependence with others.

At the end of each day, take time to reflect on all the people you have interacted with and all the others, unknown to you, who helped make your life a little easier: farmers, truck-drivers, shopkeepers, electricity workers, factory workers in distant continents, to name only a few.

Take any object in your daily life: you will never be able to list all the beings who helped bring it to you. This is a simple yet profound practice to do throughout the day. Even something as simple as a glass of water has come to us because of the myriad activities of other beings. We were all once utterly dependent on the care and loving nurturance of our parents, our teachers and our community. None of us would reach adulthood without the continuous care and support of many people. Thich Nhat Hanh uses the word "interbeing" to describe our absolute interdependence on others.[5] Taking time to recognize and honor our web of interconnectedness every day can be a powerful technique for opening the heart.

CULTIVATING IMPARTIALITY AND UNIVERSAL RESPONSIBILITY

Equanimity means a willingness to cultivate impartiality, to see all beings as equally deserving of love and compassion. This is sometimes called the "attitude of universal responsibility."

Universal responsibility does not mean that we stop loving our family and friends deeply and passionately; it means that we are prepared to extend that love to an ever-widening circle of others in our meditation. If we don't do this then our judgments and discriminations always threaten to cut us off from others. To begin fostering this attitude, meditate on difficult situations in your life, or a place where there is trouble or conflict in the world, and cultivate the attitude of love and compassion for all of those involved.

GENERATING A FEELING OF EQUALITY

There are two simple meditation practices that the Dalai Lama recommends and promotes wherever he goes. In the first practice you simply reflect as follows: "I am one and others are vast in number. All of the other beings in the world are just like me in wanting happiness and wishing to avoid suffering. In that most fundamental sense we are exactly alike." You then contemplate the question: "If I only want happiness for me and my favored few then what sort of selfish, narrow-minded person would that make me?"[6] After deeply reflecting on this question, imagine practical ways that you can develop qualities of kindness and compassion in yourself.

The second practice is a simple imagery and visualization meditation that you can try. Settle yourself in meditation. When you are ready, imagine yourself as a neutral person. On your right, imagine your usual self, totally caught up in your own needs and desires. Take time to build these two senses of yourself as both a neutral observer and your usual self. Then imagine on your left is a group of people undergoing hardship and difficulty. Hold these images as long as you can and reflect on which of these is more worthy of your love and compassion.

Remember, this is a mental practice to build some muscle into your understanding of equanimity, it is not about being harsh or critical or unkind to yourself!

CULTIVATING LOVE AND COMPASSION THROUGH THE REPETITION OF A SIMPLE PHRASE

The phrases I have found most helpful in cultivating love and compassion are: "May I be well and happy. May all beings be well and happy." You can use these phrases very simply in your meditation by linking them with the in-breath and the out-breath. As you breathe in, silently say in your mind, "May I be well and happy." As you breathe out, silently say in your mind, "May all beings be well and happy."

This is a simple and eloquent practice. You can do it for a few minutes at the end of each session of meditation. You can also do it anywhere at any time in your daily life, for example while sitting on a bus or just walking down the street. The point is to keep familiarizing the mind with the wish of love and compassion so that over time it will flow as a spontaneous wish for others.

You can make this practice more elaborate if you wish.

First of all, imagine as you breathe in and affirm the wish for yourself that you are drawing in all the limitless love and compassion of the world, from the highest, most sublime source you can imagine. It flows into your body, your mind, and your heart, filling you with the warmth of love and well-being. Again and again, with each in-breath you imagine opening your whole being to receive these blessings.

Then with each out-breath you simply imagine yourself joining with this universal energy and sending the wish of love and compassion out from you to all beings with increasing power and energy. You might also like to specify certain individuals who are experiencing difficulties, or places in the world where there is great suffering and hardship. Imagine as strongly as you can that all these beings individually receive everything they need for their happiness and well-being.

You can use your imagination to increase the power of this meditation further by imagining the wish of love and compassion flowing on a streaming golden light. As you breathe in you silently say, "May I be well and happy." That wish flows into your whole being on a streaming golden light, especially into your heart. As you breathe out, the wish, "May all beings be well and happy" flows out from you, especially your heart, in all directions as a streaming golden light.

A further extension is to imagine the streaming golden light of love and compassion to be coming from a numinous source or a holy being you invoke in the sky a little in front of you or above the crown of your head. Feel as strongly as you can your connection to this powerful or divine source of the streaming golden light. It comes into you on the in-breath, filling your body and mind; then you share it and send it out on your out-breath.

If you have a good imagination you can add one more dimension to this meditation.

While the golden light is streaming through your heart, imagine the bud of a beautiful, perfectly formed white flower at your heart. I like to use the image of a lotus flower, but you can use any white flower that appeals to you. The image of the bud acts as a symbol of your deepest inner potential to develop a heart of greatness. As the golden light streams through your heart on the in-breath and the out-breath, the petals of the flower bud slowly open to reveal beautiful golden stamens at its center.

When the flower is fully open, imagine that the stamens radiate some of the golden light out through your body in all directions. From the crown of your head down to the tips of your fingers and toes, your whole body is filled with this golden light of love and compassion. You can also imagine that any disease, exhaustion or depletion is purified as well. Every space, every organ, every cell in your body is suffused in this golden light of love and compassion. Imagine that your mind is also filled with its sparkling golden luminosity.

Then, before you finish your meditation session, imagine that the beautiful white flower at your heart slowly closes back into a bud. Anchor the bud in your heart with a stem so that you can return to the image in meditation whenever you wish.

You can simplify this meditation for everyday use. Wherever you are and whenever you remember, take a moment to look at the people around you—in the street, in the supermarket, on public transport or driving past in their cars. Look clearly at them, remind yourself of their fundamental similarity to you, and in your mind silently send them the wish, "May you be well and happy." Share the wish again and again, with the next person, and the next person and so on. Do this whenever you remember, person after person. You might like to make a commitment to keep reminding yourself to do this throughout the day, whenever the opportunity presents.

This wish is the constant thought of all the holy beings. Whenever we do this practice, which is a form of meditation in action, we are emulating the ceaseless compassionate activity of the awakened ones. If you like you can simplify the phrase even further to a silent, "May you be happy," sharing it with everyone around you, person by person.

FOUR TRADITIONAL PHRASES FOR CULTIVATING LOVE AND COMPASSION

In committing ourselves to the conscious cultivation of love and compassion, we need to be patient and diligent and resist the pull toward sentimentality or inflation. This requires a steady commitment to slowly saturate our mind with the idea of love and compassion so that the mind becomes completely familiar with it. In this practice we endeavor to train our minds to respond spontaneously with the thought of love and compassion. In fact, we deliberately cultivate new core beliefs and attitudes in our subconscious minds through practices like this.

In one tradition the practice is simply to repeat phrases of love and compassion over and over without the need to generate the feelings we associate with these wishes. In session after session of meditation the mind is filled with these powerful phrases. The following four phrases are said to cover all the aspects of loving-kindness:

May you be free from danger.
May you have mental happiness.
May you have physical happiness.
May you have ease of well-being.

In meditation you slowly and persistently reiterate these four phrases while steadfastly holding the image of a person in mind. Utilize the phrases in a way that feels right for you. Repeat them one after another in a round, or focus on just one of the wishes, or repeat each one for as long as it feels appropriate. The method you choose will depend on what you feel is most needed by the person who is the focus of your meditation.

Always start this practice with yourself, then extend it to an ever-widening circle of people and ultimately to all forms of sentient life. It is considered most powerful to do this practice with specific individuals in this order: self, benefactor or teacher, parents, family, loved ones, friends, strangers, difficult people, then universally to all beings.

If you do this practice regularly for yourself and others in your life, even for strangers, you will begin to notice a change in yourself. People frequently report to me a softening of previously hardened attitudes and prejudices, a new lightness and generosity of heart and mind. I strongly recommend that you try it. Don't be in a hurry. Always start with yourself and do it slowly. Stay with each individual for quite a long time: for weeks, months or possibly even years with some of your really challenging "precious jewels" (as the Tibetans call their most difficult antagonists!). If you do it diligently enough, you will begin to notice over time quite strong feelings of friendliness when you meet, or even think of, the people whom you are individually holding in your meditation this way.

At the start, individualize the words for yourself: "May I be free from danger. May I have mental happiness. May I have physical happiness. May I have ease of well-being." When you start, just do it for yourself. Then, when that wish is stable, bring in another person. Do it for yourself and them. Then later add another. You can then develop your own individual way of doing this meditation, adding people and letting them go out of the practice as your confidence develops. Try to hold as vivid a mental image as you can of each person as you do it for them.

TWO TECHNIQUES FOR DEEPENING THE CULTIVATION OF LOVE AND COMPASSION

FRIEND, ENEMY, AND STRANGER MEDITATION

Our usual habit is to see people as having fixed, inherent qualities. In our mind we tend to keep them stuck in a role: as a friend (one whom we cherish and care for); as an enemy (one toward whom we feel animosity, anger, irritation, resentment, or even hatred) and as a stranger (one for whom we rarely spare a thought). The following practice is designed to break down the solidity of these categories in our mind.

When using this meditation method, first settle yourself by thoroughly relaxing, then rest your awareness on the movement of the breath for a few minutes. The formal practice begins with a focus on yourself. Gently turn your full, affectionate attention to yourself, holding yourself close and dear in the same way that you would hold a very dear and close friend if they were present. Send love and warmth to yourself: acknowledge that most of the time you do your best. Rejoice in your achievements and be kind and forgiving about your shortcomings or failures. Continue to do this in a loving and kind way for two or three minutes.

Next bring to mind a friend and hold their image in your mind's eye as vividly as you can. Take a few moments to build the image in as much detail and with as much feeling as you can. Rejoice in all their good qualities and how they enrich your life, and feel your willingness to overlook their failings. For a while, bask in the warm feelings their image brings up and send them your love, your care and your wish that they receive every possible blessing. Continue to hold their image in your mind's eye as strongly as you can.

After a few minutes, let the image of the friend go and bring to mind the memory image of a neutral person, someone you do not know well. It could be, for example, someone you regularly pass in the street or who serves you in a shop. Hold their image as vividly as you can. Then remind yourself that this person, like you, wants to be happy and not suffer. This person has friends and loved ones, dreams and plans; they too are prone to the fears, worries and pressures of life that affect you. If you got to know this person you would see all these aspects of their life. On the basis of this reflection, generate feelings of warmth and kindness toward this person for a few minutes.

Let go the image of the neutral person and bring to mind the memory image of a difficult person in your life, called an "enemy" in this practice. (It's wise to not start with your most difficult person, a betrayer or abuser; it may take a good deal of time and patient practice before you are able to work with them.) Make it only a *slightly* difficult or irritating person in your early attempts at this meditation. Once again, hold their image in your mind's eye as vividly as you can. Feel your resistance, your unwillingness to hold them in this way.

Then take some time to generate other thoughts about the person: "I only experience the deluded and difficult aspects of this person at the moment. Things could change, enemies often become friends and friends can become enemies. If I knew this person in a different setting they could easily be a friend. How foolish to let the mere circumstances of my life prevent me seeing the positive qualities in this person. This person is just like me in their fundamental desire to have happiness and avoid suffering." On the basis of this reflection try to send them warmth and kindness. Wrap them in your best wishes for a few minutes.

While you are holding the image of the difficult person in your meditation you may like to experiment with the possibility of forgiveness as well. Reflect as follows: "No matter how the pain, unhappiness or suffering came to me from you, I forgive you. I forgive you for what you did and didn't do, in your actions, your speech and your thoughts."

Just experiment for a few moments with the possibility of forgiveness between you and this person. If you are feeling courageous you might like to add the following: "And however hurt or suffering came from me to you, please forgive me too. Please forgive me." Remember to make it *unconditional*; this is the only way that a forgiveness practice can shift hard, resistant resentments in the mind. You require nothing back from the other person. You are trying to cultivate the wish because you want to, because you are sick of living with the harshness of resentment wrapped around your heart.

After a few minutes of working with the difficult person or "enemy" in your meditation, let go of their image from your mind. Notice how you feel and how difficult it was, and cultivate the resolve to keep doing this challenging practice. It's good to take a minute or two to finish the meditation with a more general wish: that all the beings in the world find a way to let go of their habitual judging minds, find relief from their sorrows, grief, suffering and sadness, and cultivate love and compassion.

USING AN IMAGE TO HELP CULTIVATE LOVE AND COMPASSION
Over many years I have found the following images helpful in supporting my meditation practice. You might find them interesting to experiment with and helpful in your meditation, particularly if you have trouble generating a feeling of love in your meditation.

Generate a mental image of someone from your past who loved you deeply, generously and perhaps even unconditionally. It may be a parent, a grandparent, a neighbor, an aunt or uncle, a teacher or a dear friend. Most of us have had at least one such person in our life. Choose one of these people and take time to recover the memory of them in all its rich, feeling tones. Do this as vividly as you can.

Then imagine you are in the presence of this person. Try to feel as strongly as you can the love and tender regard flowing from them to you. Give yourself time to bask deeply in that remembered love. Then, while you hold this image in your meditation, kindle the same feeling deeply inside yourself, in your heart and mind. After some time, when you have gained confidence and solace in this practice, experiment with using one of the meditation techniques to share compassion and love described in this chapter.

Another helpful technique is to use your imagination in meditation to build an image of a mother tenderly nursing her small, precious child. See if you can build that image clearly in your mind's eye. If you did not have a loving mother, you can perhaps recall the example of motherly love you have seen in other families or in the great Renaissance paintings. When you can hold this image, imagine that a wise, motherly part of yourself is lovingly holding and nurturing you as if you were your own small, precious child. Give this tender and most nurturing affection from you to you. Allow yourself to bask in your love in this way, holding yourself close and dear. If there has been a dearth of love and kindness in your past, this meditation can provide a powerful image to help open your heart and begin to feel the quality of love and compassion you have yearned for.

A simple practice to help lighten your mood and soften the hard edge of judgment, resentment and anger in the mind is to practice *smiling* while you meditate. It is hard to stay angry, sad, depressed, or unloved if you are smiling. You may need to shift old, entrenched habits of cynicism, sadness, or despair at the ways of the world. At first you may feel inauthentic, as if you are faking it. Willfully holding a gentle half-smile in the corners of the mouth can be enough to help you move toward a softer, more loving disposition. When used over time, this can be a great help in cultivating the attitude of love and compassion more consciously in your meditation sessions.

In all of the meditations for cultivating love and compassion, it is important to start with yourself. The importance of doing this was eloquently expressed by the Buddha when he said, "You can search throughout the entire universe for someone who is more deserving of your love and affection than you are yourself, and that person is not to be found anywhere. You yourself as much as anybody in the entire universe deserve your love and affection."[7] Most of us are not good at doing this!

BREATHING OUT NEGATIVITY

In this practice, after settling and composing yourself, imagine that you are sitting in a vast open plain. In front of you is a gate. Let the image of the gate take whatever form spontaneously arises in your mind. Create an air of expectancy. When you are ready, imagine that the gate slowly opens outwards. This is an invitation to you to let go all your fears, worries, hurts and anger, and any other negative energy in your heart and mind. Gently breathe these hurts and negative thoughts out, one at a time. As the out-breath passes through the gate it is immediately transformed into the golden light of universal compassion. This golden light then flows out into the vast plain all around you, which is filled with sentient beings in human form. The golden light of universal compassion gives to each being what they need for their healing and transformation.

The meditation deepens as you continue to breathe out all your negative emotions and experiences and see each one instantly transformed into universal compassion as it passes through the gate. Do this meditation for as long as you like, simply releasing and letting go of more and more of your negative emotions and experiences, imagining them immediately transformed.

At the end of the meditation, imagine that this golden light of universal compassion has satisfied all the needs of the numberless sentient beings around you and circles back to fill your own heart and mind as well. Before you finish, take time to rest in that feeling.

BREATHING LOVE

In the second meditation, again imagine yourself sitting in a vast plain. This time your father is sitting on your right, your mother on your left. All of your friends and loved ones are sitting behind you; all your enemies and difficult people in front of you. The area all around, out to the horizon, is filled with sentient beings in human form. For a few moments, imagine how it would be if you could extend your small quota of love and compassion to all of these beings. Try to stay relaxed and easy, not overwhelmed by the task.

When you are ready to proceed, begin by fostering a deep loving acceptance of yourself. Imagine yourself filled with love and compassion. You can imagine it coming from your deepest wisdom energy, from a memory of a powerful love you have experienced, or from the inflowing love and compassion of a holy being that you visualize in front of you or above the crown of your head. Take time to build a sense of the energy and vibrancy of this love and compassion in every part of your body and mind. As this love fills you, imagine it effortlessly flowing out of you—firstly to your loved ones, then to the difficult people, and finally to all beings. Take your time: it will take practice to make this meditation wide and expansive.

You can send a range of wishes flowing out with your love and compassion; for example: "May you dwell in your heart. May your fears and sorrows fall away. May you find the healing that you seek. May you be happy and may all your experiences be good. May you experience peace and joy. May you have a long life and quickly achieve your highest potential. May all your suffering cease and may your mind be happy and peaceful."

THE PRACTICE OF GIVING AND TAKING

This is a traditional Tibetan meditation for extensively developing the good heart. The practice was widely used in Tibet by great yogis and adepts and has traveled to the West with the Tibetan diaspora that followed the Chinese invasion and annexation of Tibet in 1959. There are an increasing number of excellent translations of traditional Tibetan texts that explain this meditation in detail, and many living Tibetan meditation masters have also written extensively on this practice.[8] I introduce this meditation here to give you a taste of a practice that will both challenge and extend you in developing the qualities of the good heart in your meditation.

You might also find this meditation referred to as the practice of *tonglen*. It is a very challenging meditation practice; because of that it has enormous potential to transform the mind and generate more altruistic levels of love and compassion. At first this meditation can seem unimaginably difficult and even absurd. It is counter to what we normally do. It is also the reverse of many other meditation techniques for healing and transformation.

The essence of this practice involves mentally cultivating the thought of taking to oneself the suffering, pain and hardship of another and giving to them all your possessions, good qualities and virtues. First settle yourself in meditation, relax the body, and cultivate the most extensive motivation to help others that you can imagine; then focus your awareness on the flowing movement of the breath for a few minutes. Imagine either a person, a situation or an aspect of your own experience that involves suffering, hardship or difficulty.

Imagine that hardship as a dark, heavy, black energy, and breathe it in from that person or situation. As you do this you will initially feel resistance—after all, who wants to take on more pain and suffering? Imagine that resistance as a black knot of self-cherishing at your heart. By breathing in the black, heavy quality you are taking from the person or situation you smash the black knot of resistance and self-cherishing and liberate all your good qualities, which then go out to the person or situation on the out-breath as a light, spacious quality. The light you imagine breathing out and giving to the other person contains all that you can imagine giving them from your own resources to help heal or transform their situation.

When you first try this meditation it is a good idea to start with a scary or painful experience in your own life. After practicing it for yourself, slowly and gently move on to other people and situations. Keep on taking and giving on the breath: in with the heavy, dark energy of suffering; out with the light, spacious gift of your best possible resources and qualities. When you become more confident you can be more specific: take financial crisis and send your money; take fear and send your courage and tenacity; take dying and give your life; take disease and give your health.

I cannot imagine a harder meditation than this practice of giving and taking. I encourage you to try it, but do it for only a few minutes at a time at first. It will teach you a lot about your own resistance and those deeply conditioned and difficult places in your psyche. It has the power to open your heart in deep and unexpected ways. It directly challenges the sense we have about ourselves as limited beings with only a small amount of love to give: only enough for our own loved ones, if we're lucky. It's the perfect meditation practice to match the age-old wisdom that we cannot heal or transform in a vacuum; that our own healing is inextricably linked to the healing of others.

My teacher, Lama Zopa Rinpoche, is keen that we teach this practice to people with cancer and other life-threatening illnesses.

At first I did so with great trepidation. Many people found it too hard and put it aside to try again later. But for some it has offered an exquisitely tender pathway into previously locked places in their heart.

I am still deeply touched when I recall the awesome inner development in a woman with a most serious and painful malignancy who regularly used this meditation. In our weekly healing meditation group she frequently kept us spellbound with her accounts of reconciliation, forgiveness and healing, which flowed from her embrace of this meditation practice. I think it can be said of this woman that she healed into her dying.

chapter 9
Meditations for Health, Healing, and Managing Pain

In this chapter I outline a range of activities and meditations that you can use to help deal with illness and disease, and significant episodes of physical or emotional pain. In chapter ten, I outline some simple practices for the many other crises and problems that can threaten to unravel your life. Such crises can arrive suddenly and can be overwhelming if you are not prepared!

By sampling the strategies and meditation techniques presented in these two chapters, you will be better prepared when a major health problem or crisis occurs. If you have done a little homework beforehand through your meditation practice you may have the tools to prevent yourself being swept away in despair, isolation, unremitting sadness, blame or depression. It is possible but harder to start trying to introduce these practices when you are ill or feeling overwhelmed, or when your life feels out of control.

But just reading about these practices as interesting possibilities or good ideas is not enough. You need to select one or more of the techniques and begin to practice them, using them on the small day-to-day problems and disappointments in your life. This will stand you in good stead for the future.

There is a wide selection of possibilities here, but you cannot practice them all. One of the biggest pitfalls for people who are either on a spiritual path or seeking skillful ways to develop their inner resources is to overload themselves with too many good ideas and practices. Don't try to do too much—especially if you are ill, because your resources will be even more depleted. The wisest course is to start in a small, manageable way; build your understanding; and slowly widen your meditation practice as you become more skilled and confident.

As you read through this chapter and the next, try to feel which of the activities and meditations really speak to you. It is a good idea to pause, shut the book, and practice that particular technique for a while. If it seems to offer you a tool to help you deal with a difficult situation in your life, make a commitment to work actively with it for a few months before reviewing whether it has helped you. Otherwise it will be just another of the myriad good ideas you have already come across.

When you have done that for quite a long time, you need the courage to work out how to deepen it in your own life. Find your way of doing it. Make it an integral part of your own unique journey of awakening. If you don't internalize and personalize the practice in this way it's just another good idea you got from someone else. Aim to give the practices you embrace your own voice and inflection. This way there is every chance they will support you no matter how tough the circumstances of your life become.

The meditations set out in the earlier chapters are presented as part of a deep and continuing commitment to calming and training the mind. In this chapter and the next, the meditations are designed to help you focus on and achieve specific goals. They are best developed using as a base the meditations I have described in the earlier chapters. This can help prevent the intense, furrowed-brow striving that I have seen many people fall into, where the body becomes tense and tight and the mind is steeped in a background anxiety: "I've got to get this right," "I've got to do it" (so I don't die, or suffer, or feel pain). It's hard to imagine that it will be very effective if you practice a powerful method of healing or transformation for half an hour a day and spend the other twenty-three and a half hours in dread, anxiety, and fear!

The best base for these practices is regularly cultivating deep relaxation and mindfulness in a daily meditation practice. In deep, conscious relaxation practice you learn how to be patiently and lovingly in your body. With a regular practice of mindfulness you learn how to bring all the experiences of your life gently into your meditation. The practices in this chapter and the next will help you to deal with some of your more challenging life experiences in more specific and focused ways within your regular meditation practice. They can also help to widen and extend your meditation. After all, to be really useful, meditation should be able to help us better manage all the events of life, especially those that worry us, that throw us off balance and disturb us with very strong emotions and reactions.

There is now a large body of theory and research, with tight, well-constructed studies, in the field of mind-body medicine. This research supports what the mystic traditions have been saying for millennia: that our thoughts affect our bodies as well as our minds. The body is always listening to the mind. Every thought produces a cascade of subtle hormones, peptides and other body chemicals that speak in their own unique ways to the cells and tissues and organs of the body. If we understand this we can consciously choose to focus on the kinds of thoughts, feelings and emotions that will reinforce our goals.

We can program our thoughts to change our mind: if we continuously put in the message we want, the subconscious mind registers and holds that message. It is further argued that it is the subconscious mind that is in a direct relationship with the healing systems of the body. It is the subconscious mind that holds all of our beliefs and attitudes, and they can be changed and reshaped by our willingness to repeat and reinforce our new goals constantly.

If we regularly hold an idea, an image or a feeling in our mind, over time it will gain the force of an inner belief or conviction. When the mind is patiently trained in this way, over time there will be an increasing likelihood of more spontaneous actions in accord with that new inner belief. An image held powerfully in the mind, especially when the mind is calm, peaceful and focused, continues to grow and build even when we are not doing our formal meditation practice.

MEDITATIONS FOR HEALTH AND HEALING

I am not proposing that the meditation practices presented here are the only things you need to do, or that they can replace the best medical and other health-care support you can access. In recent times there have been a large number of biographies, self-help books and magazine articles published, telling the stories of people who have experienced extraordinary and unexpected healing in the face of serious life-threatening illness. The authors of these books and articles usually thank their loved ones and friends, their doctors and nurses. Most of them then go on to describe qualities they were able to cultivate within themselves, which they feel were equally important in their healing and recovery. Often they ascribe their healing to rediscovering the power of hope and love and to their ability to harness their willpower or a force that came from deep within themselves, which they feel was aligned with something larger and more universal than themselves.

The question is, Can we train ourselves to do this or is it only open to the fortunate few who are able to access extraordinary inner resources? I believe that we can learn to access this healing power because the potential is within us all. To balance that, we also need to understand that we are *not* "in charge"; that there is a kind of force in our lives as well. However, if we are going to be able to access and draw on these inner resources we have to be willing to do what one of my first teachers, Lama Yeshe, used to urge on all his students: Think big. We have to be willing to grant some grandeur and magnificence to our life, to affirm that "I am worthy of healing."

In this section I set out some meditations that can help with health and healing. These are presented under two broad categories: general imagery-based meditations and meditations and practices with a specifically spiritual focus. There are many other meditations you can try, but the ones I include here represent some of the meditation practices that clients and friends of mine have found helpful.

IMAGERY-BASED MEDITATIONS FOR HEALING

SPECIAL PLACE MEDITATION

In this meditation you use your imagination to create a mental picture of a place that feels special to you. It may be a real place or an imaginary place, or a real place that has your own imaginary elements added to it.

When you first do this meditation it can be a little like going through a mental filing cabinet. It's worth taking your time and being patient until you get the mental image of a place that feels right for you, a place that feels like your special corner of the universe. As you build a clear and stable image of this place in your meditation it can become a special place of healing for you, but this might take you quite a few sessions of meditation.

To begin this meditation, take time to establish your focus and motivation, compose yourself with some simple relaxation and settle your attention for a few minutes with a mindful awareness of the breath. This will help you to build the image of a sanctuary in your meditation practice. Then, when you begin to form the image in your mind, be very clear that this is a special place, a place of refuge and healing.

Take enough time at first to build the detail as clearly as you can. Look around inside your special place. Note what is in the distance, then in the middle distance and lastly what is close by. Be very clear about where you are in this imagined place and what you are doing. Feel the textures of the place; be aware of its smells, its sounds. Feel the breeze and the sun; experience its weather and any events that are happening.

The goal over time is to be able to effortlessly create this special place in your mind's eye so that you can take yourself there as often as you want. Every time you go there you can be calmed by its ambience and imagine its healing qualities filling your whole being. In your meditation you can rest in your special place, soaking it up, for as long as you wish.

Every time you return to this special place in your meditation it will become stronger and more powerful for you, like returning to your own special corner of the universe. When you become confident and familiar with this meditation you can then invite any powerful sources of healing that you can imagine to manifest themselves in that place and add their healing qualities or presence.

INNER WISDOM MEDITATION

In this meditation you invite your own deep wisdom to take a form that you can spend time with and converse with. It is helpful to be curious, alert and even a little playful when you try this particular meditation. You may be surprised by the image or images that spontaneously arise when you do a meditation like this. It is important that you do not force or manufacture an image of inner wisdom that accords with a fantasy or belief you hold. Remember that some people will be able to do a practice like this effortlessly, while others might never have a very clear or vivid experience. If nothing happens at first, keep persevering for a while with a curious and expectant attitude. You also need to be wise enough to say to yourself, "This is not for me" and try one of the other meditations in this chapter.

This inner wisdom process is best done as part of a focused time of meditation. It is important to compose and settle yourself first, as described in the previous meditation. You can invite your inner wisdom to simply manifest within the quietness of your meditation. However, you may find it more helpful first to imagine yourself in your special place, taking time to build a firm sense of being in that place.

When you are ready, take a little extra time to create a sense of expectation and then invite your inner wisdom to manifest. You can imagine that a figure starts coming toward you out of the distance or you may find it easier to simply become aware of the figure that represents your inner wisdom suddenly being present. Let it take whatever form it will. For some people it is a wise old man or woman; for others it is a child, a person from the past, a parent or grandparent, an archetypal being, a cartoon character or even an inanimate object. When I first did this exercise I experienced it as a huge rainforest tree that spoke to me.

I've always found it helpful to do this exercise by first imagining that I have climbed up to a mountain peak or onto a high plateau, with the expectation that I will meet my inner wisdom in that elevated location. To try this, imagine that you are in a natural setting, such as walking through a forest toward a mountain you are going to climb. Take time to climb the mountain through a variety of terrains and gradients. When you reach the top, take time to imagine looking out at the huge vista before you. Sit and rest for a while. When you are ready, imagine your inner wisdom manifesting to meet you in that spacious, elevated place.

If you want to have a conversation with this wisdom being, be prepared to ask your questions and then allow the conversation to unfold as easily as you can. Don't force it. Be prepared to ask your questions in different ways if you are uncertain or unclear about the answers you are given. Be interested in whatever comes. The answers and general comments made by the inner wisdom beings in these meditations are usually quite simple. You can ask if they have any general advice. When it's time to finish you can also ask if you can come back and seek their help when you need it again. The conversations are usually quite brief.

Some people use this kind of meditation regularly, but most people find it is something to do only occasionally, when they feel in need of some deep inner guidance. Remember to keep this meditation simple. There's no right way to do it. Don't give up if you don't achieve the visualization easily, but don't force it either. The inner wisdom figure must be a spontaneous creation of your unconscious for it to be effective. Don't be influenced by what others report. Your experience will be unique and pertinent to you, so it is a good idea to keep the experience to yourself.

USING SYMBOLS TO EMPOWER THE HEALING PROCESS

In this form of healing meditation you use your imagination to create symbols that represent your immune system and your disease or form of ill health. The environment where the action takes place represents your body. You can also imagine ancillary symbols, for example symbols for your treatment, medication and supplements that serve to strengthen and support the main symbol of your own healing energy. Before you begin, take time to go into a deep, peaceful meditation.

Then choose a symbol that represents your healing system or immune system. This symbol should be strong, powerful, vigorous, and untiring. In contrast, the symbol you choose for the disease is weak, ineffectual, and disorganized. However, this may be a problem for you if you have a sense of your disease or illness being quite strong, so you may need to make this symbol quite powerful in order to register its force in your life. Most importantly, make sure that the symbol for your immune system is stronger and more powerful than the symbol for your illness or disease.

Imagine a process in which the symbol of your immune system engages with the symbol for your disease and destroys it, flushes it away, removes it or transforms it, so that the disease is completely eliminated. It is central to the effectiveness of this meditation that the process is complete and the symbol of the illness is completely overcome. Continue to repeat this symbolic process in your meditation, imprinting it daily onto your subconscious mind. The possible scenarios and the kinds of symbols you use are as wide as your imagination, but they must be as pertinent to your situation, and the process as powerful as you can imagine.

When you are doing this form of meditation, it is best to check the details with a friend or meditation teacher to make sure that the symbols and process are clear and powerful enough to achieve the desired outcome. It might also be helpful to make a series of drawings of your symbols and the process whereby they meet, with the immune system symbol overcoming and eliminating the disease symbol. Remember that sometimes you can use the additional aid of symbols that represent your treatment and the medicine or nutritious food and supplements you are using. Our subconscious mind takes these images, the symbols and the process quite literally, so it is important that they are simple, clear and effective in conveying the outcome you want. It is important that you do not use a meditation like this if, as far as you know, there is no active disease in your body.

In this form of meditation it is best to try to generate your own symbols. Use symbols that spontaneously arise and then be creative in the way you work with them. Let the symbols and the process evolve and change over time. You may need to strengthen and increase the power or even the amount of your immune system symbol to combat an increase in the symptoms or progress of your actual disease. You need to be creative and adventurous when using this method of meditation for your healing. You also need to know when to stop doing it. For example, if you are finding it hard to have any enthusiasm for the meditation or the symbols aren't very clear or energized then it may be time to stop and do something else.

I have been privileged to have had hundreds of cancer patients describe their unique symbols and processes to me over the years. Recently a man with a serious and unexpected spread of a malignant cancer asked me to help guide him in meditation so that he could develop his own personal symbols. During the meditation he spontaneously came up with an image of his cancer as a teeming mass of pillbugs and millipedes under a large rock that had just been turned over. Then he imagined a flock of magpies descending to devour them all. This symbolic process was very effective and powerful for him and he enjoyed repeating it throughout the day as part of his regular meditation practice. He enjoyed daily the pugnacious presence of magpies in his suburban garden. When I spoke to him a few months later he said he was not using the symbolic process any longer. It had served a useful purpose, he said, but now he wanted to go deeper with his meditation practice.

We use symbols in this way because healing is still a mystery: patients with identical disease situations can experience widely varying outcomes. Also, if we try to imagine the healing process literally we may either overlook some vital component in the process or get it completely muddled and wrong. If you are unable to come up with a set of symbols that are powerful enough or if you are not sure that you currently have any active disease in your body you should try the meditations in the next section.

USING ARCHETYPAL OR UNIVERSAL SYMBOLS OF HEALING IN MEDITATION

An archetypal symbol is one that resonates with many people across boundaries of culture, ethnicity, and gender. Streaming light is probably the most universally used symbol of transcendent presence and healing energy. I have described in detail a meditation using the symbol of light in chapter two. Other examples of archetypal symbols that can help with healing are the ocean; mountains; rainbows; the sun and the moon; the clear night sky; a temple; vast open spaces with a distant horizon; a wise white-haired old man or woman; a giant oak or an ancient gnarled tree; and totemic animals like lions, whales, dolphins, bears, and snakes. Of course, many people like to use specific spiritual images like a cross, Jesus, Mary, Buddha, Green or White Tara, or Kuan Yin.

You can use a universal or archetypal symbol that is meaningful to you, in your meditation, to create a feeling of being in the presence of the most powerful and awesome universal energy you can imagine. When you have established a feeling of that invoked presence you should take time to build a feeling of personal connectedness with it. When you feel ready, request or invite the healing power of the presence to flow into you. It may take you a few sessions of meditation to do this confidently, so be patient as you build familiarity and trust in this process.

The universal or archetypal image should be connected with the highest source of wisdom, power, and energy that you can imagine. This does not have to be a religious or spiritual image. Many nonreligious people have described to me images of special places in nature, or abstract symbols that have been very powerful and effective for them when they have used this form of meditation. The connection you make with your choice of image should feel very powerful. The practice is to imagine the energy of healing, purification and transformation streaming from the source into you. As it flows into you the healing energy extends out into all parts of your body. Any disease, pain, depletion or injury in your body is immediately transformed by this energy.

You can imagine this energy as a form of light, a physical sensation or vibration, or a flowing liquid feeling. Some people prefer to imagine breathing the healing energy into their lungs at first and then they imagine it flowing out into all the parts of their body. Others find it more powerful to imagine the energy flowing downwards from the crown of the head or even upwards from the soles of their feet. Another variation is to imagine the energy spontaneously flowing in through all the pores in your skin.

You may experience an immediate sensation of being filled with healing, like turning on a light switch in a darkened room, or you may experience a slow filling sensation as the healing energy gently flows out through the body. Some meditators imagine their disease being immediately and dramatically eliminated, whereas other people need to feel a slow, measured process in which they imagine the disease or pain being steadily transformed or eliminated from the body.

You can imagine breathing out the disease or pain as a dark, smoky substance or having it slowly flushed out of the body. Remember to let your imagination create the image for this transformation or elimination process that feels most powerful for you. In either case, try to imagine the material that is eliminated from your body either disappearing out through the atmosphere into space or down through an opening in the ground into the bowels of the earth.

There are clear, helpful, and practical ways to do healing meditations using archetypal and universal symbols, and I have described complex practices as clearly and simply as I can. It's good to be clear about what you are going to do when you start a meditation session. However, there is no "correct" way to meditate.

You will gain the greatest benefit from these meditation practices if you take time to investigate which combination of images feels most powerful for you. It can be counterproductive to force yourself to follow rigidly or adapt to an image that has been described in a recording or book. If you are using a recorded guided imagery process, please trust and follow whatever spontaneous variations emerge. Just use the taped instructions as a background to support your meditation time.

Meditations that invoke a powerful source from which flows a healing stream of light or nectar are probably the most universally used healing meditation practices. The great benefit of these meditations is that they are not complicated and don't require a complex belief system. You can also use a meditation such as this initially to invoke a powerful healing source; rest in it for a while and then imagine directing it or requesting it to flow to a loved one, friend, distant person or any place in the world where there is suffering and pain. It can be a very helpful antidote to feelings of powerlessness and fear when friends and loved ones are sick or troubled or when you hear about a terrible catastrophe.

MEDITATING ON AN IMAGE OF YOURSELF IN GOOD HEALTH

It is powerful to take a few minutes before you end a meditation session to sit with an image of yourself in perfect good health with all your illness and disease gone. Take time to develop this image to make it as vibrant as you can.

For example, imagine yourself doing something you really enjoy which you may not have been able to do for some time: walking your dog on a beach, hiking in the mountains, playing with your children, dancing with your friends. This is like giving your inner healing systems a blueprint of what you want to achieve. Imagine you are speaking to all your immune system cells, saying, "This is what we are aiming for, go for it!" You can make it even more powerful by imagining yourself when you are fully recovered, doing things to help others who may be suffering a similar health problem to you.

CULTIVATING IMAGES TO CONNECT WITH YOUR INNER RESOURCES

In his book *Wherever You Go, There You Are*, Jon Kabat-Zinn outlines two meditations, using the image of a mountain and a deep still lake, to help build feelings of strength, courage and resilience.[1] The idea is to build a mental picture of a great towering mountain or a deep, peaceful lake. When you have a strong picture in your mind's eye, explore all its qualities in detail and then imagine that you can become like that mountain or lake, with all its qualities. A mountain is such an imposing presence in the landscape. Weathered by storms and seasonal changes over millennia, it continues to sit as a still and calm presence in the environment. A deep mountain lake always has a calm stillness in its depths no matter what is happening on the surface. We can use these images in meditation to cultivate the same qualities of calmness and inner strength within ourselves.

In other meditations you may imagine going on a healing journey, passing through a series of powerful archetypal environments and experiences that are connected with deep feelings of well-being. The possibilities are endless: climbing a mountain; sitting on a promontory that juts out into the ocean; walking in a high alpine meadow or somewhere like the vast Tibetan plateau; being in a mountain forest surrounded by towering trees; flying like a great soaring eagle; swimming in a warm tropical pool under a waterfall; lying in the dappled light beside a flowing stream.

Take time to build a healing story or journey through a sequence of images that resonate most strongly with you. Ask your friends or loved ones to help you develop this sequence, but don't judge these sequences with your normal critical mind. Sometimes the stories that play out are quite naïve, even gauche. If these images or stories come up spontaneously or keep insistently presenting themselves be willing to use them and be curious to see what happens.

USING IMAGES FROM YOUR MEDITATION IN DAILY LIFE

During times of ill health or disease it is powerful to find ways to extend the images of healing you use in meditation into your daily life. The following examples will give you the idea of how to do this yourself.

> While showering, imagine the water washing away all your disease, which flows down the drain until it is gone. Take time to imagine, as vividly as you can, your body completely healed and well.

> Before going to sleep, request your inner wisdom to help guide you by presenting dreams you can work with.

> As you go to sleep invoke the protection of a very powerful source for you: God, an angelic host, or the buddhas and bodhisattvas.

> On a hot day, imagine the sun's powerful energy healing your illness.

> When it is raining, imagine the rain purifying and cleansing you and your whole environment.

> Every time you turn on a light, use the act to imagine you are bringing light into your life and the whole world.

> Imagine your surroundings as a beautiful heavenly place or a pure realm.

> Transform every drink you take into healing nectar and all the food you eat into medicine.

> Imagine transforming any treatment you need to have, for example surgery, radiotherapy, physiotherapy, or a vile-tasting medicine, into a form of universal healing energy. Practice embracing all your treatments.

As you walk and go about your daily chores, keep coming
back to a mindful embrace of each activity every
moment.

Don't waste any opportunity to continue to train and transform
the mind!

Some books on healing present meditations using colors and
energy associated with the chakras and the subtle wind energies of
the body. Meditations using these more esoteric ideas can be very
confusing at first and I suggest you use them cautiously. If possible,
try to get specific individual instruction from a reputable, experienced and trustworthy guide if you are going to try these types of
meditations. Remember to keep it simple when working on your
healing. Life is already mysterious enough without unnecessarily
complicating it further.

SIMPLE SPIRITUAL PRACTICES TO COMBINE WITH HEALING MEDITATION

For many people the experience of an illness is a time when they
strongly connect with a religious or spiritual direction in their life.
This may be the case in your own life. I present here a few very general practices that I have observed people use, from which they
have found great strength and support.

Christians have many prayers and practices that invoke Jesus,
Mother Mary or a Saint of the church as an intercessor and protec-
tor. In the Eastern Orthodox Christian Church there is a widespread
practice of ceaseless immersion in the "prayer of the heart." These
traditional practices can be enhanced and strengthened when they
are done as part of a sustained meditation with an emphasis on calming and quieting the mind. Other practices can also be enhanced
when undertaken with a meditative approach—for example, specific
church healing services and Eucharists, anointing with oils, hands-on
prayer and focused-healing prayer by a church community. Many
people I have worked with have found great consolation in knowing
that they are on the weekly prayer lists of churches and prayer groups.

Churches and cathedrals are wonderful environments to meditate in. One client described to me how she does one of her daily meditations in Saint Patrick's Cathedral in Melbourne because it is close to her place of work. However, if it is too busy or a service is in progress she goes across the road to Saint Peter's Anglican Church. This is a lovely example of ecumenism in action!

Many years ago a cancer patient from a small country town in New South Wales described to me how the Uniting Church minister gave her a set of keys to the church so that she could go there to pray and meditate whenever she wanted. She had advanced cancer and didn't consider herself to be a practicing Christian. In fact, during her meditation she regularly invoked Sai Baba, an Indian holy man, because she had read about him and felt inspired by him. My client felt that being able to regularly sit and meditate in that quiet, sanctified space contributed to her healing, and as I write this many years later she is still living an active life. Finding a special and sacred place for your meditation can be of great help, even if you only go there occasionally.

I have met many devout Christians who have centered their meditations on such simple practices as the Lord's Prayer, the Twenty-third Psalm, a simple Latin or Aramaic word or phrase, or even a line from a favorite hymn. The idea is to use your meditation practice to enhance your invocation of divine presence. Imagine it manifesting in the most powerful sense of a felt presence that your imagination can create. As you continue to do your practice you rest simply in that invoked presence as calmly and peacefully as you can. The Christian Meditation Community is a growing worldwide group of meditators who use as a mantra the Aramaic word *Maranatha* which they translate as, "Come Lord, come Lord Jesus." The mantra is repeated softly in the mind for the duration of the meditation session. The founder of this modern revival of meditation within the Christian Church, Dom John Main, said that the purpose of the mantra meditation practice is to be with God rather than speak to God.[2]

The Tibetan Buddhist tradition that I have studied has powerful practices invoking buddha emanations—such as Tara the savioress;

Chenrezig (Kuan Yin), the bodhisattva of compassion; and the Medicine Buddha—which many people find helpful. These practices combine prayer, generation of compassion, visualization, and mantra recitation. There are many simple commentaries on these practices and most large Buddhist centers offer initiations into them. (Most Buddhist centers have meditation rooms available for anyone to use.)

Tibetan Buddhists believe there is great value in making prayers and prostrations before a holy object like a stupa or statue of a buddha. There is also said to be great value in making offerings of incense, light, flowers, fruit and other food. It is said that the quality of your meditation will be enhanced when it is preceded by prayers, prostrations, and offerings. These prayers can be very powerful when they come from a hurt or broken place in you.

You can also be supported and strengthened by attending group meditation practices, teachings and formal religious ceremonies. All of these external practices can be helpful in cultivating a spiritual path, but the greatest offering we can make to the buddhas is our willingness to practice meditation diligently and regularly to calm the mind, generate compassion and train in wisdom.

Every spiritual path offers opportunities to engage in healing activities. You may request an appointment in your preferred spiritual tradition to see a priest, rabbi, lama, vicar, or monk for advice on meditation and other spiritual practices that may help you. You can ask them to be a mentor or spiritual friend to help you with regular guidance during your time of crisis.

A dear friend of mine was given very specific and detailed meditation advice by a Tibetan lama when she fell ill with secondary cancer more than ten years ago. She left all her usual comforts of home and meditated intensively in the country for a few years. She did many other things to support herself but she believes that specific guidance and advice was one of the things that helped prolong her life.

MEDITATIONS TO HELP MANAGE PAIN

The possibility of experiencing intense and unrelieved physical pain is a universal fear. Unrelieved pain can be a frightening and all-encompassing experience. We are fortunate that medical science has developed powerful modern analgesics and opiates to help alleviate severe pain. There is of course a cost in the often debilitating side-effects of these drugs. Many people want to maintain a high level of function and consciousness through an illness. To do this it is helpful to have strategies to help increase our pain threshold and our ability to tolerate and manage pain, and meditation can be a very helpful tool for this. Pain is an intensely personal experience and it has both objective and subjective components. Relaxation, meditation, and imagery techniques can be very helpful to manage the subjective experience of pain.

Most of us can recall intense experiences of pain from the past. Our memory of physical pain is generally associated with serious injury or illness. For many women, it may be the pain of childbirth. If you can recall the episode of pain you may also remember how the experience was associated with an instinctive tendency to tighten, to clench up, and resist. Over time this habit of resistance in the presence of pain becomes entrenched. The habit of clenching, tightening, and resisting tends to exacerbate the intensity and experience of pain. The opposite reaction is one of softening, relaxing, opening and letting go. All meditation techniques designed to help with pain have this as their goal. Four broad groups of meditation strategies are frequently used: relaxation, breathing techniques and mindfulness, distraction, and focusing on the pain itself.

RELAXATION

Relaxation techniques are relatively easy to teach and to master. They offer a direct and simple method of softening and releasing as an alternative to the instinctive response of tightening and holding on. There can be a direct and immediate benefit for people experiencing difficulties with either acute or chronic pain.

If you are supporting a person with pain and offering to guide them through a relaxation process, it is very helpful to give good, clear instructions and take your time. You need to be skillful in matching your pace, language, and tone of voice to the actual expressions and behavior of the person you are working with. It is very hard to learn a new technique or to remember much detail when you are in pain. Repetition, support and steady encouragement are the keys to building confidence. A guided relaxation tape can also be helpful. Chapters four and five contain detailed explanations about relaxation strategies.

BREATHING TECHNIQUES AND MINDFULNESS

Breathing techniques and mindfulness meditation can be powerful and effective in helping to manage pain, but they require great application and they are often too challenging or paradoxical to someone already mired in pain. They are excellent strategies to persevere with if you have someone to help reinforce and support the practice. The breathing techniques are outlined in chapter six, and suggestions for using mindfulness in the management of pain are detailed in chapter seven.

A helpful variation on the breathing techniques is to imagine yourself breathing into the place in your body where you are experiencing pain or discomfort. As you breathe in, imagine the flowing, billowing energy of the breath entering deeply into your body to the place where the pain is. Imagine the breath is warm and peaceful or that it has some other quality you feel would help alleviate the pain. As the in-drawn breath touches the place of pain, it draws from it the distress and hurt, which then flows out with the exhalation. This can be very helpful when done over and over with the simple unforced rhythm of the breath.

It takes time and practice to build confidence with breathing techniques and mindfulness meditation. It is wise and very skillful if you are not experiencing pain at the moment to begin practicing now, in anticipation of what might come your way in future. Practicing patiently with the small pains and discomforts of everyday life helps to build competence and the confidence to work with the bigger pains when they arrive.

DISTRACTION

Some meditation techniques use distraction as a method to help remove awareness from what is happening in the present moment. Distraction techniques are great for children because their imagination is so alive and rich. Music, familiar stories, hypnosis, massage, *reiki* and the distraction of attention through the use of imagery can all help to raize a patient's pain threshold.

The imagery techniques on pages 129 to 139 can help you build an image strong enough to distract you from the experience of pain. Many people create a mental image of a special, peaceful, safe place, a place of refuge, to provide them with an escape from the insistent pain in their bodies. Once again, it is important to let your own imagination guide you to build images that offer peace and solace. If your pain is intense ask a loved one or friend to help by talking you through a sequence of distracting images or the rich colors and tones of a special place. This may offer some respite and relief. You may also find support from recorded guided imagery techniques, ambient sounds, and music.

When caring for a person in pain you may need to be more creative and experimental. Many patients experiencing acute or intense, unrelieved pain have told me that the music, books or self-help strategies which were once a source of support and inspiration for them no longer provide any relief. Your willingness to be a loving presence who can stay to help support and witness the situation for a friend in pain may be the best (and only) thing you can do.

In those situations you can be supported enormously by your own meditation practice. You can do visualization practices and make prayers on their behalf, but the greatest gift of a long-term meditation practice will be your ability to keep your awareness unflinchingly in the present and your heart open no matter what happens.

FOCUSING ON THE PAIN

It takes much energy to sustain a process of distraction, and the time comes when the tape stops, friends leave or it is difficult to sustain a clear mental image. Distraction techniques are useful for acute short-term pain, but for more chronic or drawn-out experiences of pain, focusing on the pain itself seems to offer better long-term relief.

It is deeply paradoxical and challenging to make your pain the object of your meditation, and it takes courage to even try. This is suggested in the folk wisdom that says you can only truly let go of something once you have accepted it. If we seek to change, avoid, or overcome something we get caught in a constant reactive stance to it. The thing we are in conflict with seems to set the agenda. By turning toward our pain and experimenting with the possibility of opening to it, no matter how painful that is initially, we cut through the habitual pattern of reaction. I have already discussed this possibility in chapter seven.

In meditation the most profound method for focusing on pain is to do the exact opposite of what we normally do. Normally when pain is present, our every thought and wish is for it to go away. This tends to create tension, clenching and tightness in our body and mind. The pain solidifies in the body and may send out ever-expanding ripples of pain and discomfort into surrounding tissues and organs. The opposite is to practice cultivating an attitude of softening, releasing and accepting whenever pain is present. It takes practice and some gritty courage but the results can be amazing. Remember, it is advisable to train yourself to do this by starting with small pains whenever they are present.

When pain is present you can do this type of meditation on its own or in combination with the breath and physical touch. On its own it is like practicing simple motherly love from you to the painful place in your body. Hold this place of pain in high awareness, tenderly, like a mother holding a small crying infant, and whisper gentle words of encouragement and kindness down into your body: words like softening, releasing, melting, loosening, flowing, letting go. You can combine these simple words, or other similar words and phrases, with a soft warm breath, which you imagine breathing down into the place of pain with every inhalation.

You can also experiment with placing your hand or hands over the place where the pain is in your body. The warmth and tenderness of that simple touch can be very healing in itself and it also provides a point of focus for the breath as you breathe it in. It is as if your touch can help pull the healing breath more palpably into the place where you are experiencing the pain.

An even more challenging practice is to use your imagination to create in your meditation a dialogue with the pain. Some people have a gift for this kind of practice. Once you have focused on creating an open, accepting relationship with the painful place in your body you can ask it questions. For example, "Why are you here? What do you want from me? What would it take to help you be calm and settled?" These suggestions are very broad; you may have questions more specific to your situation. It is not for everyone, but try it and you might be very surprised by the result.

MEDITATIONAL BODY SCAN

The "meditational body scan" is a widely used pain management technique that combines a direct focus on the pain with imagery and breathing. I first learned this technique working with Ian Gawler and we used it extensively with cancer patients. Quite a lot of patients with advanced malignancy reported that it was the only self-help technique that helped them establish a measure of acceptance and rapport with an otherwise unbearable pain. This meditation uses your imagination to create a specific shape that represents the pain so that you can then observe it and work with it. In essence, it allows you to get some distance from the pain. The meditation involves a scanning technique and a set of simple steps that you can slowly repeat over and over until there is a shift in your experience of the pain.

At the beginning it is helpful if you can find a quiet place to either lie down or settle into a comfortable sitting position. Most people in pain seem to get maximum benefit doing it lying down.

Settle yourself and take a few deep breaths to both relax and pre-pare yourself for the meditation.

Start by scanning through your body looking for any place where there is pain or discomfort. Begin at your feet, slowly scan up through the whole body to the crown of the head. If there is pain in more than one place, always focus on the place where the pain is most intense.

After you clearly identify the location of the pain in your body, very slowly and carefully allow a shape that represents the pain to form in your imagination. The shape is located in your body at the place you experience the pain and it now represents the pain. The shape should not be the literal shape of the organ or tissue involved, but something more abstract. Some common examples are a box, a ball, an oval shape, a rectangle, a spiky angular object, a rod or a corkscrew. Patiently and with real curiosity and interest identify as many details as you can about the shape: its dimensions, density, surface texture, temperature and color. The key to this meditation is to do the scanning and detailed observation of the shape very slowly and attentively, as the details may vary each time.

When you have ascertained all the clear details about its shape in your imagination, including where it is located in your body, imagine drawing the breath down into your body to gently wash around and through the shape. You are not trying to force the breath in any way. Instead, you simply use the natural cycle of the breath, actively imagining that it can flow deeply into your body to the area of pain and out from it on the exhalation. I suggest you try to do this for nine rounds of breathing, but experiment for your-self with as many or as few breaths suit you.

You can repeat the whole scanning, observing and breathing technique many times. Each time go back to scanning through the body and be curious about what you find. The pain might be in the same location but the shape might have changed. The pain may have shifted location, there may be a new pain or there may be no noticeable pain at all.

Whatever you find, simply observe it and continue to work through the process of building an abstract image of the pain once again, unless of course the pain has completely gone away. Sometimes the shift in the experience of pain can be immediate and dramatic, but at other times you may have to keep scanning and going through the whole process step by step many times before you experience a perceptible change in your pain.

This technique will not work for everybody, but if it works for you then you have a simple strategy to return to whenever your pain sharpens or intensifies. The great advantage of this technique is that instead of having to create an entire distraction scenario again and again, you can use this technique to top up your continuing strategy of observing and engaging with the pain rather than flinching and fleeing from it. It can be a wonderful aid to help remind you to soften and relax in contrast to the deep habit of tightening and resisting.

chapter 10

Meditations for Transforming Difficult Situations

My meditation teacher, Lama Zopa Rinpoche, has a very simple and much repeated piece of advice for all his students: If you have problems, don't waste them.

In his understanding, when things are going well we tend to motor along blithely, using up our accumulated good fortune. It is not until problems come and disturb us that we have a chance to wake from our usual dream-like stupor and begin to practice meditation. Meditation is primarily about working with the mind, and the great mystic traditions teach that our mind contains the seed of divinity—what is called "Buddha nature" in Buddhist teachings. This is the ultimate possibility of transformation that the great traditions speak of. We beginners on the path can start to mimic the possibility of that great transformation by actively seeking to use our meditation and mindfulness to transform the small but often very difficult challenges that are present in our daily lives.

Most of us tend to use our meditation practice in two ways. Firstly, if we are fortunate we find a connection to a great tradition that speaks of a path: of awakening, or *samadhi*, bliss, enlightenment or the heavenly realms. That taste of a sublime goal inspires us for a while and then we slowly forget, lose the vibrancy of that initial inspiration, perhaps become cynical and doubt the possibility of a transcendent experience. Then, each time we reconnect with a great teacher or have a painful experience of suffering or a private moment of numinosity, we again lift our focus to the inspiration of the highest, most sublime possibility that the tradition we are connected to speaks of.

However, most of us spend our time immersed in the stuff of daily life: establishing our careers; caring for our families and friends; putting food on the table; dealing with aging and health; worrying about the world and the fate of our children, the poor, and the dispossessed; and having fun when we can. The struggle is to maintain a regular meditation practice while also giving our full attention to all the many demands and delights that life presents.

Transformation implies a willingness to set a big goal for yourself; it does not mean using your meditation practice to merely alleviate, manage, or placate your problems. Spiritual transformation through meditation contains an invitation to keep yourself alive to the possibility of an opening and awakening in an ultimate sense, and the commitment to foster in yourself the tools for bringing about small transformations in daily life. It means not being habitually caught in the pull of greed, ignorance and hatred.

In this last chapter I outline some simple meditation strategies that help you begin the long and arduous journey to transform the difficulties and disappointments of daily life into a spiritual path.

TEN SIMPLE PRACTICES FOR DAILY LIFE

1. be skillful in your daily practice

Review your daily meditation practice constantly; seek the regular guidance of your meditation teacher if you have one. Don't let your meditation practice become mechanical. Cultivate a willingness to bring your problems into your daily practice. Make sure there is a time to do this. Be very careful not to just stick a convenient "correct-line" solution over your life's problems and hope they will go away—they won't! They will simply go down deeper inside you and fester. A friend of mine has an elegant and uncomplicated solution for the problems in her life: "I take them to the cushion" is her most often repeated statement. That is, her practice is never to flinch from a problem but to take it into her daily meditation and "chew" on it for as long as is required. So don't be surprised when problems, afflicted mind states and intense emotional reactions come up—they are not hindrances to your path, they are the path.

The Buddha said that our minds have been out of control for millennia so we shouldn't expect to tame them easily!

2. dedicate time to your problems

Dedicate a period of time in your daily meditation practice to meditate on a problem or an issue that dominates your life and holds you back. Don't be in a hurry: it may take months, years, even decades, to achieve a deep and lasting breakthrough. And don't move on from it until you feel some change in your otherwise fixed and deeply conditioned habit. Meditate on the problem in a positive, insightful way, not in a way that endlessly reconnects with your perceived failures, defeats and betrayals. It will be even more helpful if you consider some wise teachings each day and reflect on your problem in the light of those teachings.

3. pay attention to what disturbs you

Be very attentive to the seductive illusions that can hide behind your spiritual interests and meditation practice. When something arouses you in a negative way or causes a reactive response, pay attention. Work against the desire to project your response onto another person or onto the external situation. Don't just cover the disturbance and the response it elicits with a pious platitude or a spiritual slogan. Instead, cultivate the difficult habit of reflecting in your meditation on why you respond in that way. Ask yourself, "What afflictive mind state in me is being triggered here?" Situations and other people are never as we think they are. Investigate rigorously and honestly the state of your own mind: that is the only place you can really make a difference.

4. practice a reflecting meditation each day

Practice a short reviewing and reflecting meditation at the start and end of each day. At your first waking moment, rejoice in the fact that you are still alive and once again recommit yourself to cultivating your best qualities during the day. Then, when you are lying in bed or having a shower or drinking your morning cup of tea, cast your mind forward to the day and reflect on what is to come. Prepare yourself for any difficulties or complications you anticipate. If you have to deal with a difficult person, think ahead to the likely situation and send some warmth, kindness and equanimity to that person or situation.

At the end of the day, develop the habit of quickly reflecting on the day. Ask yourself, "How did I do?" Briefly recall the people you have had contact with and the events of the day. Rejoice in what you have done well and set to rights in your mind anything you feel you did badly. In doing an evening reflection like this you can momentarily touch the memory of each person with the thought of love and compassion. Another way of doing this is to sit quietly for a few minutes before you go to bed and recall each person you met from the start of the day to the end, one by one, and wish them happiness.

5. record your insights

Have a notebook with you when you meditate. If a helpful insight or idea comes up, especially if it is insistent or important, quickly note it down, then go back to your main practice. It is common to have "creativity attacks" while you are meditating and it is a pity to waste the insight or spend the rest of the meditation time trying to hang onto it. The function of your notebook is simply to record the compelling thought or insight so that you are free to return your full focus to your meditation practice.

If you keep a journal or do some daily creative or artistic activity, keep it separate from your meditation practice. While your meditation practice will inform those creative and reflective activities, be aware that they are different. It is very important to learn to trust the invitation into stillness and non-doing that is at the heart of all meditation practice.

6. contemplate on a chosen quality

If there is a quality that you would like more of in your life, set aside ten minutes each day to contemplate and reflect on that quality.

For example, it might be contentment, courage, optimism, joy, calmness, friendship, assertiveness, strength, forgiveness or self-acceptance. In your ten-minute contemplation, think of as many examples of that quality as you can. Recall them as vividly and in as much detail as you are able. Your examples might draw upon people you know who have that quality; famous people who exhibit the quality; films, books, poems, songs, folk sayings, and stories in newspapers and magazines that express it; characters in films or novels; holy scriptures; dictionary definitions; and memories of past times when a particular quality has been present in your life.

Each day, take ten minutes to connect with all the possibilities and flavors of this quality. Continue to practice this contemplation for as long as you feel the absence of the quality in your life. You may need to practice for many months. Be patient. Remember to be creative and inventive, bringing to mind each day a different aspect of the quality that you had not thought of before. When you have familiarized your mind with this quality, over time you find it easier to seek it out in other people and situations and to express it yourself.

7. cultivate antidotes to afflictive mind states

In the Buddhist tradition there are powerful teachings about the qualities we can cultivate as antidotes to afflictive mind states. You might like to learn to understand the antidotes to the afflicted thoughts, feelings, and emotions that affect your life, then cultivate these antidotes in your daily meditation. You can do this in a similar way to that described for contemplating on a quality.

Some of the main antidotes detailed in the Buddhist scriptures are patience (the antidote for anger); equanimity (for attachment); rejoicing (for jealousy); moderation (for greed); courage (for fear and anxiety); generosity (for meanness); forgiveness (for resentment); compassion (for indifference). The antidote is generally the opposite to the way we normally behave.

When you are clear about the right antidote for your afflicted mind state, use your meditation practice regularly to rehearse situations where you act in accordance with the antidote. Also reflect on situations where you returned to your old habits and forgot to apply the antidote. In your meditation practice, contemplate on some wise teachings about the value and importance of the qualities contained in the antidote.

When you work with a specific antidote to any afflicted mind state, do so unconditionally and because you want to have that particular quality in your life. Let go of the idea of life as a contract, where you endlessly recycle a mental list of what you owe others and what they owe you. A sentiment I often hear is, "I'll forgive them when they say they are sorry and do what they should have done." The practice of cultivating an antidote in your meditation relies on a willingness to do it *regardless* of what other people do.

Remember to apply the antidote when the strong mental affliction is present. Because we habitually justify our emotions, this is not easy to do. You will be more likely to succeed if you become familiar with the antidote in your regular meditation practice.

8. make time for reflective meditation

Most spiritual traditions have a collection of core teachings that an aspiring student is instructed to reflect on in a systematic and regular way. Make time for reflective or analytical meditation in your regular meditation practice. Alternatively, set aside time each day or a few times each week for uninterrupted study, contemplation and meditation. Christians might make time to study the Gospels or Psalms; Buddhists may take a section of the Dhammapada or a sutra to contemplate.

In the Tibetan tradition, there is an attempt to codify the essence of the Buddha's path into a set of topics that are collectively called the *Lamrim*, or stages on the path. A student can take many years to work through each topic, doing a reflective and analytical meditation on one, or a small part of one, each day. This is a wonderful way to internalize a great wisdom tradition and to deepen your understanding of it. The goal is to have that wisdom available so that you can effortlessly recall it when needed.

9. cultivate friendships

Finally, we are all helped to grow up into mature, adult human beings by the loving and kind support of others. We grow best with faithful and loving partners, families, friends, teachers and mentors, and a community that values us and to which we feel connected. Not everyone can get all these riches in their life. You may need to find a wise teacher or mentor, and this may require a long and arduous search. Sometimes we have to reach out humbly to friends we have neglected, or take the risk of trying to extend a friendship into a deeper level of openness and intimacy.

I have been very fortunate in having a loving partner and many good friends. Among these are a few friends with whom I go for regular long walks. These times of close friendship have been tremendously important to me and on those walks we sometimes fall into a wonderfully quiet and contemplative reverie together. I hope that you will also have the good fortune to find some strong and true friendships in your life. Remember that these friendships have to be nurtured and supported. It takes time and requires trust and a willingness to be patient, open and vulnerable. These are also qualities required to sustain and deepen your meditation practice.

10. practice contemplative meditation

There are two contemplative meditations that I use to jolt me out of complacency. I describe them here for you to consider as well.

In the first meditation, put aside about half an hour. After settling yourself carefully, take as much time as you need to build the following image: you have just returned from a visit to your doctor, who has told you that tests have confirmed you have a very advanced terminal illness and are going to die in three months' time. (Remember that this is a fantasy exercise and bears no relationship to your actual situation.)

The power of this exercise comes from your willingness to build the sense of shock, fear and grief that such a diagnosis would evoke. Imagine as vividly as you can that you are going to die in three months' time with no negotiation and no reprieve possible. The one positive thing is that you will be in good health right to the end, and then you will die. What will you do in that three-month period?

Spend the rest of the meditation time contemplating how you would use that time, then come up with a list of at least ten things you would do. Before you finish the meditation, prioritize the items in your list. At the end of the meditation, write these ten things down on paper or in your journal.

If you do this meditation with a strong intent and focus you may be surprised by what comes up. I try to do this meditation at least once a year. I have found it very helpful in making sure I've got my priorities right. Once you have written your list, reflect on it and ask yourself why you have to wait until you are dying to do these things if they are so important? Keep this list in your diary or journal and reflect on it regularly in the coming months.

In the second meditation, again set aside at least half an hour. In the silence of meditation reflect on the question, "What are the ten most important things in my life?" Take your time doing this. Make sure that you cover all aspects of your life: family, career, reputation, spiritual aspirations, friendships, possessions, relationships, health.

When you have done this, write these ten things (or more) in a list. Prioritize them, with the most important first. Go back to your meditation and imagine as vividly as you can what your life would be like without the item at the end of the list. Take your time. Then do the same with the second last item. Do this very slowly, all the way to number one on your list. How would your life be without any of these things being present? It's like doing a "Who am I?" exercise in reverse: "When I remove these things, who am I?" This meditation challenges us to ask, "Without all the things on my list, is there anything left?" You may find that your priorities change after you do this exercise.

You need to do this exercise compassionately, slowly and conscientiously. If you do not feel increasingly pained and bereft as you strip these things away, you probably don't have the right list. In this meditation you must slowly and deliberately work with each loss.

These two meditations, and the one that follows below are not designed to alarm or frighten you. Rather, they cut to the heart of our human condition and they allow us to register more directly the alarming truths of impermanence and death. No matter how secure, comfortable and safe we are now, circumstances can change suddenly and dramatically. In a moment, all our resources and certainties can be taken from us.

We all benefit from a steady daily meditation practice to build the kind of inner resources that will strengthen us to cope with a sudden emergency. We will all die one day and be forced to leave all these things, and much more, behind. The aim of these meditations is to remind us of what we know and yet daily forget. We can't suddenly decide to forgive our worst enemy or abuser if we haven't worked on forgiving our small daily problems.

Following below is one of the most challenging—and most powerful—meditations of all.

EXERCISE

EMBRACING THE REALITIES OF LIFE AND DEATH

This meditation, though it may seem depressing, is one of the most important and life-affirming practices you can engage.

Set aside fifteen to twenty minutes to do this guided death contemplation. It is based on a traditional Buddhist practice called the Three Roots, the Nine Reasonings and the Three Convictions contemplation. Take a couple of minutes to pause and contemplate each point.

Death is certain. There is no possible way to escape death. Each moment brings me closer to my dying. Death comes in a moment and its time is unexpected. Cultivate the conviction to develop a practice that will ripen your inner potential.

The Time of Death is uncertain. The duration of my lifespan is uncertain. There are many causes and circumstances that lead to death. The weakness and fragility of my physical body contributes to life's uncertainty. Cultivate the conviction to ripen your inner potential, now without delay.

The only thing that can help me at the time of my death is my inner development. At the time of my death, worldly possessions can't help me. My relatives and friends can't prevent my death or go with me. Even my precious body is of no help to me.

Cultivate the conviction to develop the conviction required to ripen your inner potential purely, without stinting in your efforts.

glossary

bodhisattva ~ One who possesses the altruistic wish to achieve full enlightenment in order to free all beings from suffering and bring them to enlightenment.

buddha ~ A fully enlightened being. The historical Buddha was Buddha Shakyamuni or Prince Siddhartha Gautama who lived in India six hundred years BCE.

buddha nature ~ In Buddhist philosophy it is asserted that every sentient being possesses the potential to become a fully enlightened buddha.

Buddhism ~ One of the great world religions that is based on the teachings of the historical Buddha, Shakyamuni Buddha. Buddhism is broadly divided into two schools: Theravada (practiced in Sri Lanka, Cambodia, Thailand, Laos and Burma) and Mahayana (practiced in Tibet, China, Mongolia, Japan, Vietnam, Korea and Siberia). Mahayana, or the Great Vehicle school, encompasses the Pure Land and Zen traditions in China, Japan and Korea.

chakras ~ The psycho-spiritual energy centers found in the body along the central channel between the crown of the head and the sexual organs. The main chakras are the crown, throat, heart, navel and sacrum.

enlightenment ~ Full awakening or buddhahood: the ultimate goal of Buddhist practice. It is a state characterized by unlimited compassion, skill, and wisdom.

Four Noble Truths ~ The essence of the first discourse of Shakyamuni Buddha after his enlightenment, and the foundation of Buddhist teaching. The Four Noble Truths are the truth of suffering; the truth of the origin of suffering; the truth of cessation; and the truth of the path.

lotus posture ~ The cross-legged sitting posture common to Eastern meditation traditions. Some traditions speak of the "full-lotus posture" which requires considerable flexibility and involves resting the top of each foot on the opposite thigh with the sole of the foot facing the ceiling.

mantra ~ Literally means "mind protection." Mantra involves the recitation of (usually Sanskrit) syllables associated with a particular practice or visualization.

mindfulness meditation ~ Purposefully paying attention to the present moment in a particular way, non-judgmentally.

meditation practice ~ The time an accomplished or aspiring meditator puts aside each day to do his or her formal meditation.

mind-body medicine ~ An interdisciplinary view of medicine which proposes that the mind, neurological system and immune system are all related and important in health and healing. There is a growing body of research indicating that what is happening in the mental and emotional processes of a patient often matters in the physical course of the disease.

prayer ~ Essentially prayer involves quieting and turning inward to focus on connecting with a transcendent reality or a spiritual being.

prostration ~ The practice of prostrating oneself in front of a holy object to offer humility, respect and devotion. There are two forms of prostration. In one, the hands, knees and forehead touch the floor; in the other, the whole length of the body is lowered onto the floor with the arms also stretched above the head onto the floor.

stupa ~ A Sanskrit word meaning a reliquary that is symbolic of the Buddha's mind.

subtle-wind energy ~ The subtle energy of the life force that according to Eastern esoteric teachings flows in the central channels and meridians of the body.

sutra ~ A Sanskrit word meaning a discourse of the Buddha.

tonglen ~ Taking and giving; the meditation technique of using your imagination to take on the suffering of others and give them your own happiness.

Vipassana ~ Often called Insight Meditation, the meditation practice of mindful attention. It is used to investigate and familiarize oneself with the way in which things exist in order to develop wisdom.

endnotes

PREFACE

1   Pema Chödrön, *The Wisdom of No Escape*, Shambhala Publications, Boston, Mass., 1991, p. 7.

2   This anecdote is told by S. N. Goenka in a videotape presentation shown to participants on the Vipassana Meditation organisation's ten-day retreats.

CHAPTER 1

1   M. Walshe (trans.), Meister Eckhart, *German Sermons and Treatises*, vols 1 and 2, Watkins Publishing, London, 1979, 1981.

CHAPTER 2

1   William Shakespeare, "Hamlet," act 2, scene 2, line 259, *The Complete Works of William Shakespeare*, Cambridge University Press, London, 1982.

2   Candace B. Pert, *Molecules of Emotion: The Science Behind Mind-Body Medicine*, Touchstone, Simon & Schuster, New York, 1997.

3   Ramana Maharshi, *The Spiritual Teaching of Ramana Maharshi*, ed. D. Goodman, Shambhala Publications, Berkeley, Calif., 1972.

4   Frank Lawlis and Jeanne Achterberg, "Imagery in Healing" workshop (audiotape), *Tenth Annual Common Boundary Conference*. Distributed by Sounds True, Boulder, Colo., 1990.

CHAPTER 3

1   "Whatever you can do or dream you can, begin it. Boldness has genius, magic and power in it. Begin it now." Quoted in

Susan Haywood, *A Guide for the Advanced Soul*, In Tune Books, Sydney, 1985.

2 Venerable Lama Zopa Rinpoche suggested this motivational prayer to the participants at his first Healing Meditation course at Tara Institute in Melbourne in August 1991. His teachings on that course formed the basis of his book *Ultimate Healing: The Power of Compassion*, ed. Ailsa Cameron, Wisdom Publications, Boston, Mass., 2001.

3 See Thich Nhat Hanh, *The Miracle of Mindfulness: A Manual on Meditation*, Beacon Press, Boston, Mass., pp. 27–31, on creating a day of mindfulness in your home.

4 Many resources can be found online at www.buddhanet.net.

5 Shakyamuni Buddha, The Perfect Awakening Sutra (Mahavaipulyapurnabuddha sutra).

6 Thomas Merton (trans.), *The Wisdom of the Desert: Sayings from the Desert Fathers of the Fourth Century*, Sheldon Press, London, 1961.

CHAPTER 4

1 Ram Dass, *Be Here Now*, Crown, New York, 1971.

2 Ian Gawler, *You Can Conquer Cancer*, Hill of Content, Melbourne, 1984.

3 Ainslie Meares, *A Better Life: The Guide to Meditation*, Greenhouse, Melbourne, 1989.

4 There is a selected bibliography of scientific papers by Dr. Ainslie Meares on pages 148–49 of his book *A Better Life: The Guide to Meditation*.

5 Herbert Benson, *The Relaxation Response*, Avon Books, New York, 1976.

CHAPTER 5

1 Jon Kabat-Zinn, *Full-Catastrophe Living: Using the Wisdom of Your Body and Mind to Face Stress, Pain and Illness*, Delta Books, Dell Publishing, New York, 1990, pp. 75–93.

2   Desmond Zwar, *Doctor Ahead of His Time: The Life of Psychiatrist Dr. Ainslie Meares*, Greenhouse Publications, Melbourne, 1985.

3   Blaise Pascal, *Pensées*, section 2, no. 139, trans. A. Krailsheimer, 1996 (1670).

CHAPTER 6

1   Dogen (1200–1253) in John Baldock (ed.), *The Little Book of Zen Wisdom*, Element Books, London, 1994, p. 23.

CHAPTER 8

1   Gospel of St. Matthew, Chapter 25, verse 40.

2   Sharon Salzberg, *Lovingkindness: The Revolutionary Art of Happiness*, Shambhala Publications, Boston, Mass., 1995. Salzberg quotes the relevant section of this sutra on the first page of this book.

3   It is a basic foundation of Buddhist philosophy that all phenomena lack inherent existence; that is, they do not exist from their own side without depending on causes and conditions.

4   Meister Eckhart, quoted in Wayne Miller, *Sabbath Rest: Restoring the Sacred Rhythm of Rest*, Bantam Books/Random House, New York, 1999, p. 140.

5   Thich Nhat Hanh, *The Heart of Understanding*, Parallax Press, Berkeley, Calif., 1988, p. 3. See also his books *The Miracle of Mindfulness*, Beacon Press, Boston, Mass., 1975, and *Peace Is Every Step*, Bantam Books, New York, 1994.

6   This meditation and others are explained by the Dalai Lama in *The Art of Happiness: A Handbook for Living*, Hodder, Sydney, 2000.

7   Quoted in Sharon Salzberg, *Lovingkindness: The Revolutionary Art of Happiness*.

8   See, for example, Sogyal Rinpoche, *The Tibetan Book of Living and Dying*, Rider, London, 1993, and the books by Pema Chödrön in the bibliography. Pema Chödrön has also made

some excellent audiotapes on this practice. These are distributed by Sounds True, Boulder, Colo.

CHAPTER 9

1   Jon Kabat-Zinn, *Wherever You Go, There You Are*, Hyperion,
New York, 1994.

2   John Main, *Word into Silence*, Darton, Longman and Todd,
London, 1980.

bibliography

Achterberg, Jeanne. *Imagery in Healing*. Shambhala Publications, Boston, Mass., 1985.

Benson, Herbert. *The Relaxation Response*. Avon Books, New York, 1976.

Borysenko, Joan. *Minding the Body, Mending the Mind*. Bantam Books, Random House, Reading, Mass., 1988.

Chödrön, Pema. *The Wisdom of No Escape*. Shambhala Publications, Boston, Mass., 1991.

——*Start Where You Are: A Guide to Compassionate Living*. Shambhala Publications, Boston, Mass., 1994.

——*When Things Fall Apart: Heart Advice for Difficult Times*. Shambhala Publications, Boston, Mass., 1997.

Doga, Geshe. *Inner Peace and Happiness: The Path to Freedom*. Lothian Books, Melbourne, 2002.

Gawler, Ian. *Peace of Mind*. Hill of Content, Melbourne, 1987.

——*Meditation—Pure and Simple*. Hill of Content, Melbourne, 1996.

——*The Creative Power of Imagery*. Hill of Content, Melbourne, 1997.

——*You Can Conquer Cancer*. Hill of Content, Melbourne. 2001.

Goldstein, Joseph. *The Experience of Insight: A Natural Unfolding*. Unity Press, Santa Cruz, Calif., 1976.

Gunaratana, Bhante Henepola. *Mindfulness in Plain English*. Wisdom Publications, Boston, Mass., 1993.

Gyatso, Tenzin, the Fourteenth Dalai Lama. *Path to Bliss, A Practical Guide to the Stages of Meditation*. Snow Lion Publications, Ithaca, N.Y., 1991.

——*Healing Anger: The Power of Patience from a Buddhist Perspective*. Snow Lion Publications, Ithaca, N.Y., 1997.

——*Kindness, Clarity and Insight*. Snow Lion Publications, Ithaca, N.Y., 1998.

——*The Art of Happiness: A Handbook for Living*. Hodder, Sydney, 1998.

——*An Open Heart: Practising Compassion in Everyday Life*. Hodder, Sydney, 2001.

Hanh, Thich Nhat: *The Miracle of Mindfulness: A Manual on Meditation*. Beacon Press, Boston, Mass., 1975.

——*Peace Is Every Step: The Path of Mindfulness in Everyday Life*. Bantam Books, New York, 1991.

——*Anger: Buddhist Wisdom for Cooling the Flames*. Rider, London, 2001.

Hasslacher, Barbara. *Sanctuaries: Spiritual and Health Retreats in Australia, New Zealand and the South Pacific*. Choice Books and Australian Consumers Association, Marrickville, NSW, 2000.

Kabat-Zinn, Jon. *Full Catastrophe Living*. Delta Books, Bantam Doubleday, Dell Publishing Group, New York, 1990.

——*Wherever You Go, There You Are: Mindfulness Meditation in Everyday Life*. Hyperion, New York, 1994.

Kornfield, Jack. *A Path with Heart*. Bantam Books, New York, 1993.

——*After the Ecstasy, the Laundry*. Rider, London, 2000.

Lafitte, Gabriel and Ribush, Alison, *Happiness in a Material World: The Dalai Lama in Australia and New Zealand*. Lothian Books, Melbourne, 2002.

Le Shan, Lawrence. *You Can Fight for Your Life*. Jove Publishing, New York, 1978.

——*Cancer as a Turning Point*. Plume, Penguin, New York, 1990.

Levey, Joel. *The Fine Arts of Relaxation, Concentration and Meditation: Ancient Skills for Modern Minds*. Wisdom Publications, Boston, Mass., 2001.

Levine, Stephen. *Healing into Life and Death*. Gateway Books, Bath, UK, 1987.

McDonald, Kathleen. *How to Meditate: A Practical Guide*. Wisdom Publications, Boston, Mass., 1984.

Meares, Ainslie. *Relief Without Drugs: The Self-Management of Tension, Anxiety and Pain*. Collins/Fontana, London, 1970.

——*The Wealth Within*. Hill of Content, Melbourne, 1978.

Salzberg, Sharon. *Lovingkindness: The Revolutionary Art of Happiness*. Shambhala Publications, Boston, Mass., 1995.

Sogyal Rinpoche. *The Tibetan Book of Living and Dying*. Rider, London, 1993.

Thondup Rinpoche, Tulku. *The Healing Power of Mind: Simple Meditation Exercises for Health, Well-being and Enlightenment*. Shambhala Publications, Boston, Mass., 1996.

Trungpa, Chögyam. *Cutting Through Spiritual Materialism*. Shambhala
    Publications, Berkeley, Calif., 1973.
Wallace, Alan. *Tibetan Buddhism From the Ground Up: A Practical
    Approach to Modern Life*. Wisdom Publications, Boston, Mass., 1993.
——*Buddhism with an Attitude*. Snow Lion Publications, Ithaca, N.Y.,
    2001.
Yeshe, Lama Thubten and Lama Thubten Zopa Rinpoche. *Wisdom
    Energy*. Ed. Jonathan Landaw, with Alexander Berzin, Wisdom
    Publications, Boston, Mass., 2000.
Zopa Rinpoche, Lama Thubten. *Transforming Problems into Happiness*.
    Wisdom Publications, Boston, Mass., 2001.
——*The Door to Satisfaction: The Heart Advice of a Tibetan Buddhist
    Master*. Ed. Ailsa Cameron and Robina Courtin, Wisdom
    Publications, Boston, Mass., 1994.
——*Ultimate Healing: The Power of Compassion*. Ed. Ailsa Cameron,
    Wisdom Publications, Boston, 2001.

index

about the author

In addition to fifteen years of practice as a therapist and counselor, Bob Sharples has been meditating for thirty years. Since 1991 he has led stress reduction and healing courses for the seriously ill and their families, as well as for Vietnam veterans. He is married with three children and lives in Melbourne, Australia.

about Wisdom

Wisdom Publications, a nonprofit publisher, is dedicated to making available authentic Buddhist works for the benefit of all. We publish translations of the sutras and tantras, commentaries and teachings of past and contemporary Buddhist masters, and original works by the world's leading Buddhist scholars. We publish our titles with the appreciation of Buddhism as a living philosophy and with the special commitment to preserve and transmit important works from all the major Buddhist traditions.

To learn more about Wisdom, or to browse books online, visit our website at wisdompubs.org. You may request a copy of our mail-order catalog online or by writing to this address:

Wisdom Publications
199 Elm Street
Somerville, Massachusetts 02144 USA
Telephone: (617) 776-7416
Fax: (617) 776-7841
Email: info@wisdompubs.org
www.wisdompubs.org

THE WISDOM TRUST

As a nonprofit publisher, Wisdom is dedicated to the publication of fine Dharma books for the benefit of all sentient beings and dependent upon the kindness and generosity of sponsors in order to do so. If you would like to make a donation to Wisdom, please do so through our Somerville office. If you would like to sponsor the publication of a book, please write or email us at the address above.

Thank you.

Wisdom is a nonprofit, charitable 501(c)(3) organization affiliated with the Foundation for the Preservation of the Mahayana Tradition (FPMT).

Wisdom's bestselling *In Plain English* titles.
The classic guides to beginning and maintaining
your meditative practice.

Mindfulness in Plain English
Revised, Expanded Edition
Bhante Gunaratana
224 pages, ISBN 0-86171-321-4, $14.95

"Extremely up-to-date and approachable, this book also serves as a very thorough FAQ for new (and not-so-new) meditators. Bhante has an engaging delivery and a straightforward voice that's hard not to like."—*Shambhala Sun*

"Of great value to newcomers...especially people without access to a teacher."—Larry Rosenberg, author of *Breath by Breath*

Zen Meditation in Plain English
John Daishin Buksbazen
Foreword by Peter Matthiessen
128 pages, ISBN 0-86171-316-8, $12.95

"Down-to-earth advice about the specifics of Zen meditation: how to position the body; how and when to breathe; what to think about. Includes helpful diagrams and even provides a checklist to help beginners remember all of the steps. A fine introduction, grounded in tradition yet adapted to contemporary life."—*Publishers Weekly*

Meditation for Life
Martine Batchelor
Photographs by Stephen Batchelor
168 pages, ISBN 0-86171-320-8, $22.95

"*Meditation for Life* offers simple, concrete instructions in meditation and the photographs are delicious eye candy. Author Martine Batchelor spent 10 years in a Korean monastery and presumably knows a lotus position when she sees one; she also has a sense of humor."—*Psychology Today*

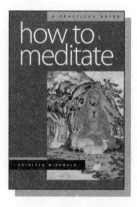

How to Meditate
A Practical Guide—Second Edition
Kathleen McDonald
256 pp, ISBN 0-86171-341-9, $14.95

"Whether you are a beginner or a seasoned practitioner, this book has jewels of wisdom and practical experience to inspire you. Kathleen McDonald comes from a long and trustworthy lineage of teachings. In *How to Meditate*, she shares the best of what she has received."—Richard Gere